D0759987

INSIGHT ⊙ GUIDES

EXPLORE

PERTH

ST AUSTRALIA

PLAN & BOOK
YOUR TAILOR-MADE TRIP

 **BRAZIL**
 **CHILE**
 **ECUADOR**

TAILOR-MADE TRIPS & UNIQUE EXPERIENCES CREATED BY LOCAL TRAVEL EXPERTS AT INSIGHTGUIDES.COM/HOLIDAYS

Insight Guides has been inspiring travellers with high-quality travel content for over 45 years. As well as our popular guidebooks, we now offer the opportunity to book tailor-made private trips completely personalised to your needs and interests.
By connecting with one of our local experts, you will directly benefit from their expertise and local know-how, helping you create memories that will last a lifetime.

HOW INSIGHTGUIDES.COM/HOLIDAYS WORKS

STEP 1
Pick your dream destination and submit an enquiry, or modify an existing itinerary if you prefer.

STEP 2
Fill in a short form, sharing details of your travel plans and preferences with a local expert.

STEP 3
Your local expert will create your personalised itinerary, which you can amend until you are completely satisfied.

STEP 4
Book securely online. Pack your bags and enjoy your holiday! Your local expert will be available to answer questions during your trip.

BENEFITS OF PLANNING & BOOKING AT INSIGHTGUIDES.COM/HOLIDAYS

PLANNED BY LOCAL EXPERTS
The Insight Guides local experts are hand-picked, based on their experience in the travel industry and their impeccable standards of customer service.

SAVE TIME & MONEY
When a local expert plans your trip, you save time and money when you book, even during high season. You won't be charged for using a credit card either.

TAILOR-MADE TRIPS
Book with Insight Guides, and you will be in complete control of the planning process, from the initial selections to amending your final itinerary.

BOOK & TRAVEL STRESS-FREE
Enjoy stress-free travel when you use the Insight Guides secure online booking platform. All bookings come with a money-back guarantee.

WHAT OTHER TRAVELLERS THINK ABOUT TRIPS BOOKED AT INSIGHTGUIDES.COM/HOLIDAYS

Trip to Portugal

Every step of the planning process and the trip itself was effortless and exceptional. Our special interests, preferences and requests were accommodated resulting in a trip that exceeded our expectations.

Corinne, USA ★★★★★

Trip to Vietnam

The organization was superb, the drivers professional, and accommodation quite comfortable. I was well taken care of! My thanks to your colleagues who helped make my trip to Vietnam such a great experience.

Heather ★★★★★

CONTENTS

Introduction

Recommended routes for...   6
Explore Perth & West Coast
  Australia   10
Food and drink   16
Shopping   20
Entertainment   22
Activities   24
History: key dates   26

Directory

Accommodation   110
Restaurants   118
Nightlife   126
A–Z   128
Books and film   138

Credits

About this book   140
Credits   141
Index   142

Best routes

1. Swan River and Kings Park   30
2. Perth Water and South Bank   34
3. City Centre and Old Perth   38
4. Cultural Centre and
     Northbridge   44
5. Subiaco   48
6. East Perth   52
7. Fremantle   56
8. Perth's suburban beaches   62
9. Rottnest   68
10. Swan Valley   72
11. South of Perth   78
12. Margaret River and
      Southwest   82
13. Southern Ocean and
      Goldfields   88
14. North of Perth to Shark Bay   92
15. Ningaloo and the Pilbara   98
16. Broome and the Kimberley   103

ART LOVERS

Perth's newest public plazas, Elizabeth Quay (route 1) and Yagan Square (route 3) both feature fantastic street art, while the Art Gallery of Western Australia (route 4) and the Fremantle Arts Centre (route 7) offer even more creativity.

RECOMMENDED ROUTES FOR...

BALL WATCHERS

With the construction of Perth Stadium, WA's biggest AFL (Australian Rules Football's top league) and cricket teams have relocated their home games to East Perth (route 6), where you can also check out the WACA and State Tennis Centre.

CAPE CRUSADERS

Visit WA's southwest corner (route 12), where the Indian and Pacific oceans meet at Cape Leeuwin. Alternatively, go north and explore Cape Inscription (route 14) or Ningaloo-facing Cape Range National Park (route 15).

ESCAPE ARTISTS

Leave the city in the rear-view mirror, hit the highways that cross the immensity of Western Australia, and traverse true deserts to discover the genuine outback in places like Bungle Bungle, Wolfe Creek (route 16) and Kalgoorlie (route 13).

FASHIONISTAS

Hit the arcades in Perth's City Centre (route 3), where chic boutiques offer fashionable threads and curious keepsakes. Fremantle (route 7) offers vintage fashion and artisan jewellery.

GOLD CHASERS

A gold trail extends around the city from the Perth Mint (route 3), but to see the source of the bling, swing along the Great Eastern Highway to the Super Pit in Kalgoorlie (route 13).

WANNABE DAVID ATTENBOROUGHS

Swim with whale sharks off Exmouth (route 15), manta rays in Shark Bay and dolphins in Monkey Mia (route 14), coo over quokas on Rottnest (route 9) and meet a mob of kangaroos on Heirisson Island (route 2).

WINERS AND CAFFIENDS

Devotees of the bean flock to Freo's Cappuccino Strip (route 7), but Perth boasts plenty of small-batch coffee roasters and artisanal brewers too. For a grape escape, head to the Swan Valley (route 10) or Margaret River (route 12).

INTRODUCTION

An introduction to Perth and West Coast Australia's geography, customs and culture, plus illuminating background information on cuisine, history and what to do when you're there.

Explore Perth & West Coast Australia   10

Food and drink   16

Shopping   20

Entertainment   22

Activities   24

History: key dates   26

Captain Cook claims Botany Bay

EXPLORE PERTH &
WEST COAST AUSTRALIA

WA is separated from the rest of the continent by deserts and the barren Nullarbor Plain. Travelling to the capital involves a long-haul flight, even for residents of other Australian cities. Is it worth the effort? Read on…

To those who have been and seen what lies hidden here, such a question is unfathomable. The tyranny of distance divided by the splendor of isolation, multiplied by stunning natural features, wonderful wildlife and a population defined by their diversity and free-range frontier mentality all adds up to produce a dramatic destination full of sensational surprises and extraordinary adventures.

From the urbane eateries and classy coffee shops in Perth and Fremantle, to the epic empty enormity of the Kimberley and Kalgoorlie, and the reef-ringed Exmouth coast, this paradisiacal place offers myriad unique experiences.

Here you can explore fine wine, kaleidoscopic coral, extraordinary art and beautiful beaches that fringe a coastline stretching 10,194km (6,334 miles) – not including the islands, of which there are over 1,000.

POPULATION AND PEOPLE

Western Australia covers 2,529,875 sq km (976,790 sq miles) and has 2.6 million inhabitants; the population density is one person per square kilometre (compared to 375 in the UK, and over 8,000 in Singapore). However, over 2 million of those people live in Perth.

An attractive, open-minded and youthful city (the median age is 36), Perth has long attracted skilled inhabitants. Over a third of the population was born outside Australia, with one in 10 originally from Britain (a legacy of the 1945–72 'Ten-Pound-Pom' programme that offered assisted passage for British citizens).

The mining boom instigated a 60 percent jump in immigration in the early 21st century, and Perth is now home to 217 different nationalities. Beside Brits, other sizable groups include Irish, Italians, Indians, Malays, New Zealanders and South Africans. Indigenous Australians form just 3.1 per cent of WA's population.

GEOGRAPHY AND LAYOUT

A behemoth state that could swallow most of Western Europe, WA stretches from the South Pacific into the Tropic of Capricorn and occupies a third of the Australian continent.

Indigenous Australians have been living here for at least 40,000 years

Perth, 14km (9 miles) inland from the Indian Ocean-facing port of Fremantle, is one of the world's remotest capital cities, closer to Singapore and Jakarta than it is to Canberra or Sydney.

Outside metropolitan Perth, the state is divided into nine regions: Peel; the wine-producing South West; the Great Southern surfing hotspot; Wheatbelt; Mid West; gigantic Goldfields-Esperance; rusty red iron-rich Pilbara; Gascoyne; and tropical Kimberley.

WESTERN AUSTRALIA'S HISTORY

First arrivals

Australia broke away from Gondwanaland 15 million years ago and drifted into its present position. Ice ages periodically lowered sea levels, exposing land bridges connecting Australia to New Guinea, enabling humans to migrate on foot. The ancestors of Australia's Aboriginal population arrived thus, about 50,000 years ago.

European explorers

Aristotle pondered the possible existence of Terra Australis in the 4th century BC, but it wasn't until 1606 that Europeans verifiably landed on Australian soil, when Dutchman Willem Jansz visited Cape York. Ten years later his compatriot, Dirk Hartog, sailed the *Eendracht* into Shark Bay and became the first European to set foot on Western Australia.

Others followed, usually by accident and with tragic consequences (none more so than the *Batavia*, see page 95) but little else happened until 1770, when Captain Cook reached eastern Australia. Land-

Indigenous people

Western Australia was populated by sophisticated people at least 40,000 years ago, as evidenced by cave art still visible in the Kimberley, such as the Gwion Gwion (Bradshaw) paintings.

The original occupants of the Perth area are collectively known as the Noongar. Before 1829, 13 separate tribes lived on land stretching from Geraldton to Esperance. However, when settlers arrived tribal numbers were decimated by disease and violence.

Farming increasingly forced indigenous people into towns or camps. In 1839, Rottnest Island became a penal establishment for indigenous people. Over 3,700 men and boys were imprisoned for offences like burning bush or digging up vegetables on their own land.

Active until 1958, the *Native Welfare Act* enabled the forced removal of indigenous children from their biological parents, especially those of mixed descent. Members of this 'stolen generation' were placed in camps at Carrolup and Moore River.

In the late 20th century, past wrongs began to be acknowledged and pressure to recognise Aboriginal land rights mounted. The 1992 High Court Mabo ruling ceded Aboriginal rights to some traditional lands, a decision ratified a year later with the *Native Title Act*.

Arrival of the first prisoners at Botany Bay

ing in Botany Bay, Cook charted 4,000km (2,485 miles) of coastline, naming it New South Wales and claiming it for Britain.

Disregarding Dutch claims and 50,000 years of Aboriginal settlement, the Imperial British – who had overflowing prisons and were looking for a foothold near the Dutch East Indies – spotted a double win. Declaring the continent *terra nullius* (an empty land owned by nobody), they claimed it and began shipping undesirables there. The first fleet of convicts arrived on the east coast in 1788.

Captain George Vancouver claimed Western Australia for Britain in 1791, landing at Possession Point and naming King George Sound (near modern-day Albany).

Swan River Colony

Fearful of French designs on Western Australia, the British sent Major Edmund Lockyer to fortify King George Sound in 1826. The same year Sir James Stirling sailed up the Swan River to the site of present-day Perth.

On 2 May 1829, the Swan River Colony became Britain's third settlement in Australia when Captain Charles Howe Fremantle planted the Union flag on the south head of the city that now bears his name. Stirling arrived with 68 settlers the following month. Perth was founded on 12 August, with the symbolic felling of a tree on a hill overlooking the Swan.

Indigenous reaction

Conflict inevitably erupted between colonists and the Noongar people, who occasionally protected their resources with force. Attacks on settlers were followed by reprisals, as was the case with the hunting down and killing of the warrior Yagan in 1833.

As governor, Stirling strived to maintain friendly relations, but after a series of violent incidents he led a punitive expedition against the Murray River people in 1834, misleadingly remembered as the 'Battle' of Pinjarra, during which a group of Aborigines, including women and children, were ambushed and shot, resulting in 30 deaths.

Around Perth the indigenous community rapidly declined, and by 1837 only 120 Noongar remained.

Convicts

Unlike New South Wales and Van Diemen's Land, WA was planned as a profit-making 'free settlement', and the British government encouraged investors with generous land grants.

By 1848, however, the colony had only attracted 41,000 people, resulting in a labour shortage. Settlers petitioned Britain to make WA a penal colony, and the first convicts arrived in 1850. Over the following decade, convict labour built Government House, Perth Town Hall, the Cloisters, Fremantle Jail and many other structures.

Gold

The discovery of gold in the late 1880s finally made Perth. Mining became the bedrock industry for city and state, and

Baby quokka on Rottnest Island

Stromatolites at Shark Bay

remains so. The first find was at Halls Creek in the Kimberley, but in 1893 three Irishmen – Paddy Hannan, Tom Flanagan and Dan Shea – made a strike that triggered a rush, opened up Kalgoorlie and made the area world-famous as 'The Golden Mile'.

Prospectors flooded Perth and business prospered. Irishman C.Y. O'Connor engineered a water pipeline from Perth to Kalgoorlie and by 1900 almost £4 million-worth of gold was being exported. People spilled into new suburbs and trams, roads, drains, sewerage and lighting were installed.

Federation

In 1890 the British Parliament passed an act that made WA self-governing. John Forrest became the first premier and the colony subsequently (albeit reluctantly) voted in favour of federation. Western Australia became a state of the new Commonwealth of Australia on 1 January 1901.

Secessionists remained vocal, though, and in a 1933 referendum 68 percent of WA voters opted for the state to leave Australia and return to the British Empire as an autonomous territory. The decision was never implemented – largely because Westminster didn't support it.

War

In World War I, nearly 40 percent of men aged 18–44 in WA volunteered. Western Australian ANZACs served again in World War II. Thousands were captured in the

---

DON'T LEAVE WESTERN AUSTRALIA WITHOUT...

Swimming the oceans. Diving into both the Indian and South Pacific oceans – and visiting the spot where these two mighty beasts collide, at Cape Leeuwin (see page 85).

Getting cultural. Finding out about WA's indigenous history and culture by visiting the Katta Djinoong Gallery in the Western Australia Museum, and the Aboriginal Galleries in the Art Gallery of WA (see page 44).

Taking in the vista across the Swan River. From the war memorial on the flanks of Mount Eliza in King's Park there is a stunning panoramic view (see page 30).

Experiencing a Sunday session. Frequent an ocean-facing bar in Freo for an ice-cold beer while 'the Fremantle Doctor' fans your face (see page 66).

Travelling back in time. Visit the earliest form of life on Earth, stromatolites, which have been around for 3.5 billion years. Find these living fossils in Hamelin Pool within Shark Bay World Heritage Area (see page 97).

Meeting a quokka. These impossibly cute cat-sized marsupials are regularly encountered on Rottnest Island (see page 68).

Going for gold. Visit the Perth Mint (see page 40) or the Super Pit in Kalgoorlie (see page 90), where enormous machines are seemingly reduced to the size of Tonka toys by the epic scale.

Mining for iron ore

1942 fall of Singapore, and Perth feared invasion for the first time, especially after the bombing of Darwin. HMAS *Sydney* was sunk off the west coast, while Broome and Wyndham suffered air attacks.

Fremantle was essential to the war effort; it was used as the secret base for 170 allied submarines with flying boats taking off from the Swan.

Victory in the Pacific (VP Day) on 15 August 1945, was celebrated in perth.

Responding to US-led concerns about the spread of communism, Australians took part in later conflicts in Korea, Malaya and Vietnam.

Boomtime

The 1950s saw a construction surge in Perth, with the completion of the Causeway and Narrows Bridges.

Fortunes were made in new mineral booms, such as nickel. Driven by a buoyant mining industry, Perth became Australia's fastest growing capital in the first decade of the 21st century, the city's population rising by 346,000.

Major projects, such as the New MetroRail and the construction of Brookfield Place (completed 2012), Elizabeth Quay (2016), Yagan Square (2018) and FOMO in Fremantle (ongoing), have all been undertaken in recent years.

CLIMATE

Perth, Peel and the coastal areas south of the Tropic of Capricorn are warm most of the year, experiencing a dry heat tempered by a cooling sea breeze (aka The Doctor) on summer afternoons. Winter (June–August) can be rainy. Inland it's hot and dry, though occasionally cold at night, and in the tropical Top End there are two main seasons: the humid Wet (December–April, when cyclones can happen) and the Dry (April–September); the latter is the best time to head north.

CULTURE AND ECONOMY

Perth's media is parochial, nightlife is low-key and Sunday trading was only recently deregulated. The city's lack of conspicuous effort is relished by Perthites, who enjoy heading to the beach and bars after a decent day's work. But this relaxed, no-worries image is deceptive: WA produces an extraordinary 46 percent of Australia's total exports.

Mining is the key, as it has been since the 19th century gold strikes. WA is one of the world's most productive mineral and petroleum regions, and the powerhouse of the resources industry in the Asia-Pacific region.

Perth's house prices and civic energy levels rise and fall like a pitching ship, riding alternate waves of boom and gloom. As the last boom faded to an echo, infrastructure and construction projects continued, but the state lost its AAA rating and unemployment rose.

However, going into 2019, a new resources boom – fuelled by LNG, iron ore, gold and lithium exports – is being heralded.

Mark McGowan, WA's Labor premier

POLITICS

Two WA politicians, John Curtin and Bob Hawke, have held the country's top job. Curtin, Australia's World War II leader, is remembered as one of its greatest; Hawke, longest-serving Labor PM, its most charismatic.

Australia's head of state is the British monarch, represented by a governor-general. The political system comprises a two-chamber parliament, the House of Representatives (elected MPs) and the Senate, where all the states have equal representation, regardless of population. Federal law made voting compulsory in 1924.

Federal parliament controls national affairs and the armed forces, but the states retain local power. Since 1986, WA has had six Labor premiers, and two Liberal. The current premier is Mark McGowan (Labor) who succeeded Colin Barnett (Liberal) in 2017.

FUTURE CHALLENGES

At its present rate of growth, Perth is predicted to have a population of 3.5 million by 2050, necessitating an estimated 800,000 new dwellings. Current plans indicate the intention is to build more intensely in places like Subiaco, rather than create more suburbs.

TIPS FOR EXPLORING WESTERN AUSTRALIA

Road kings. Give road trains plenty of space. Get over to the left of your lane when they're approaching in the other direction, and definitely don't cut them up and expect them to be able to stop.

Midweek savings. There are usually plenty of deals available on quieter days of the week. Look out for, and take advantage of, discounts such as 'tight-arse Tuesdays' at cinemas and shows.

Pack a snood. Massive swathes of Western Australia are blanketed in dusty red desert. Elsewhere these lightweight, multifunctional scarves will come in handy to protect bits of you from other unforgiving elements.

Maintain perspective. Australia is a continent-sized country and WA occupies over a third of it. Check your distances and

don't try to cover too much in a day's drive. It's better to enjoy fewer places properly than rush everywhere.

Park-up after dark. Driving any real distance between dusk and dawn is a bad idea. You'll be likely to encounter everything from big roos to feral camels on the road in Outback WA.

Bring your own snorkel and mask. WA is surrounded by the most extraordinary coastline, with gin-clear bays and, further north, fantastic coral reef. Having your own mask, snorkel and fins will open up the marine world.

Read the signs. If you see a notice warning that salt water/estuarine crocodiles are present in waterways and on beaches in the north, take heed – don't become lunch.

FOOD AND DRINK

Fine wine, boutique beer, craft coffee, fusion-food full of local ingredients, plus fruits de mer freshly harvested from two oceans – a cornucopia of tasty treats awaits the adventurous palate in Perth and WA.

Besides being one of the planet's loneliest capitals, with no sizeable neighbour for several thousand kilometers, Perth is also one of the world's most diverse cities, with more immigrants than any other Australian city and over 200 nationalities chipping ingredients, ideas and recipes into the community hotpot.

Asian, African and European influences are particularly apparent in food markets and on menus. Add to this an ensemble of dynamic chefs wedded to local produce while channelling international culinary trends, and you'll find modern Australian cuisine that rivals the food scene in Sydney and Melbourne.

LOCAL CUISINES

Western Australian food remained defiantly British until well into the 1950s. The first inklings of a Mediterranean influence gained traction in the 1920s when the first Italian and Slav immigrants arrived. But it's only since Asian immigration, the advent of fusion cuisine and the food revolution of the 1980s that the dynamic cuisine that defines the country today developed.

Such is the profusion of flavours in contemporary Perth that you'd now have to scour myriad menus to find anything akin to a staid English roast with Yorkshire pudding. These days a meal of prime WA lamb is likely to have a Moroccan or Mediterranean mien, and fish dishes will often be accented with Thai, Malay or Vietnamese verve.

Even the good old Aussie pavlova has taken a back seat to desserts such as black sticky rice pudding or coconut-fried ice cream. From risottos to rotis, sambals to sausages, every element of every national cuisine is reinvented on Perth menus every week.

Specials board

Chilli mussels, made with locally farmed shellfish, is an all-time Perth favourite, as is chargrilled marron, served with a lime beurre blanc, à la **Lamonts** – the restaurant that first introduced these indigenous freshwater crustaceans to the national table. Locals also love slow-braised lamb shanks encased in pastry, as prepared at **Darlington Estate Winery Restaurant** (see page 124).

A key feature of the local cuisine is excellent produce. Long renowned for

Barramundi is locally sourced and often seen on menus

high-quality lamb, beef and wheat, as well as fish, fruit and vegetables, the state has seen a massive increase in the production of gourmet produce. Boutique bakeries, artisan and organic butchers and specialist cheesemakers thrive, thanks to an upsurge of public interest in good food.

Farm to fork
Wagyu beef from WA's Southwest regularly finds its way onto Perth's most discerning tables, and Kervella artisan goat's cheese (made in Gidgegannup, 40km (25 miles) northeast of Perth) is now a staple on many a menu. Superbly succulent and tender White Rocks veal is beloved of the finest east-coast eateries; farmed barramundi and trout have now joined marron, rock lobster, Patagonian toothfish, sardines, dhufish and snow crab at the table.

Boutique olive oil production is at an all-time high, with almost every region in the state offering a unique blend of extra virgin olive oil. Locally grown persimmons, tamarillos and tropical fruits have joined a long list of staples, such as stone fruits, apples and pears.

Locally made chocolates and preserves can compete with overseas imports, as well as the array of artisan yoghurts on offer. Local black truffles are also now appearing on Perth's top tables.

Italian
Fremantle and Northbridge are renowned for their proliferation of Ital-ian- and Mediterranean-inspired restaurants and cafés. The fashionable suburb of Subiaco has also joined the fray, with several Mediterranean-inspired eateries, while just next door in Shenton Park you will find **Galileo**, famous for its wood-fired roast duck.

Chinese
Prospectors from China were among WA's earliest non-European settlers, and excellent Chinese restaurants are found across the state, with menus priced to suit all pockets. Although predominantly Cantonese, other regional Chinese cuisines are making their presence felt. Northbridge is known for its many Chinese restaurants. **Canton Bay Restaurant**, at the foot of Jacob's Ladder, is popular.

Thai and Vietnamese
Thai, Vietnamese and Malaysian restaurants are also abundant in and around Northbridge and to a lesser extent in Fremantle. Among the best is the award-winning **Dusit Thai** in Northbridge, the **Sala Thai** in Fremantle (see page 124), and **Lido Vietnamese** in Northbridge.

Food and drink prices

Prices for a two-course dinner for one, with a half-bottle of house wine:
$$$ = over A$40–60
$$ = A$40–60
$ = under A$40

Cicerello's

Indian

Indian cuisine is rapidly evolving into one of the most popular options in Perth, especially in the suburbs. Among the most established restaurants are the **Royal India** on Hay Street and the **Punjab** on Scarborough Beach Road.

Japanese

From upmarket teppenyaki restaurants and stylish sashimi and sushi specialists, to casual sushi and noodle bars, Japanese cuisine is amply represented. Among those that have stepped into the culinary limelight are **Tsunami** in Mosman Park, for superb sashimi and sushi, and **Nine Fine Food** in North Perth (see page 122), which is famous for combining Japanese and European flavours.

The rest of the world

Less prolific, but readily accessible, are Indonesian, Burmese, Korean, German, Mongolian, Greek, Egyptian and Lebanese restaurants. And if you still hanker after a big old British feed, many a pub will have their version of a roast or bangers and mash on the menu.

Fish and chips

Unsurprisingly, given WA's beach-focused lifestyle, fish and chips is a perennially popular option. (Be aware that in Australia, unless specified the fish in fish and chips is usually 'flake', a generic term for shark meat – potentially including endangered species, which is a growing concern.) Every seaside suburb boasts a restaurant offering the catch of the day cooked in the preferred English style, with lashings of batter and deep-fried chips, and maybe some deep-fried battered prawns and scallops for good measure. **Cicerello's** and **Kailis**, both in Fremantle's fishing-boat harbour (see page 123), are local institutions.

DRINKS

Fantastic fruit is grown in WA, from Kununurra in the tropical north to Albany on the shores of the Southern Ocean, and fresh-squeezed juices and smoothies are ubiquitous

---

Food festivals

Perth and WA people need little excuse for a shindig so food festivals are common. One of the best is Margaret River's **Gourmet Escape** (www.gourmetescape.com.au), a carnival of fine food and wine amid the vines each November. **Mandurah Crab Fest** (www.crabfest.com.au) attracts around 100,000 crustacean-munchers every March, and in June the **Manjimup Kerfuffle** (www.trufflekerfuffle.com.au) kicks off the annual truffle snuffling season. Look out for events in the Swan Valley, too.

Good times at Little Creatures in Fremantle

thirst-quenching options on menus across the state. Good quality green and black tea, as well as native bush brews and chai, are all widely available, while Asian bubble tea is popular in some places in Perth.

Coffee

Australia is now justifiably famous worldwide for its highly advanced coffee culture, and the bean scene in WA is vibrant. Perth and Fremantle both boast roasters, grinders and baristas of the highest quality. Freo has its own 'Cappuccino Strip', and Perth has enough caffeine outlets to keep you awake for life – notable options include **Mo Espresso** in Trinity Arcade, **La Veen Coffee** in King Street, and **Architects and Heroes** in Subiaco.

Beer

After decades of swilling Swan Brewery basics like Emu Bitter, the hop-heads of WA thirstily embraced the boutique beer revolution of the early 21st century, and Perth is known as the craft ale cradle in Australia. Local breweries include Little Creatures, Feral Brewing Co and Gage Roads.

Sip beautiful beer in Perth's more particular watering holes, such as **Petition Beer Corner** and **Bob's Bar** on St Georges Terrace, and **Northbridge Brewing Company**. In Fremantle the **Sail and Anchor** is soaked in craft ale history, and **Little Creatures** is just across the road (see page 123).

Even areas better known for wine are turning their talents to brewing. In the **Swan Valley** (see page 72), Mash Brewing, Homestead Brewery and Elmar's in the Valley are producing beautiful beer, and Duckstein does a drop with a distinct German accent. In the state's southwest, around **Margaret River** (see page 82), breweries like Eagle Bay, Cheeky Monkey and Bootleg are all making amazing ales.

Wines

WA boasts nine wine-growing regions and over 350 wineries, largely concentrated in its southwest corner. Though they produce just 3 percent of Australia's wine production, they account for 20–30 percent of the country's premium wines.

The most famous and prestigious region is **Margaret River** (www.mrwines.com). Renowned as a producer of robust cabernets since the early 1970s, it has since forged a reputation for crisp whites, notably chardonnay and semillon sauvignon blanc blends. Its shiraz has also won acclaim, and merlot is widely used as a blend component. Home to estates such as Evans and Tate, Cullen, Leeuwin and Pierro, and with more than 70 cellar doors, the region is a magnet for international wine-lovers.

Other areas include the **Great Southern**, **Pemberton**, **Manjimup**, the **Perth Hills** and **Swan Valley** (known for its fortified wines).

Shopping in Trinity Arcade

SHOPPING

Chic boutiques, indigenous art outlets, monster malls, atmospheric markets, urban arcades and jewellery shops offering polished, precious prizes – souvenir hunting in the wild west is an adventure in itself.

The shopping scene in Western Australia has a unique defence against online retail: it's not an experience that can be replicated remotely.

Some people who profess to hate shopping love perusing Freo and Perth's peculiar cocktail of unique boutiques, maze-like markets, behemoth malls (air-conditioned oases during summer), treasure-trove arcades and curio shops. Further afield you can explore indigenous artwork or invest in some heavy metal and shiny minerals at mine-door jewellery outlets.

ARCADES AND MALLS

In central Perth a catacomb of arcades burrows through the buildings between St George's Terrace, Hay, Murray and Wellington streets, pulling in punters of all persuasions. These covered shopping enclaves range from the ultramodern to the antique and frankly incongruous.

The latter includes **London Court** (www.londoncourt.com.au), which was built in 1937 in a style reminiscent of Elizabethan England. Stepping in from the heat of the street feels like an exercise in time travel, and inside you can do everything from visiting a cobbler to buying big-time bling, including Australian opals, South Sea pearls and Argyle diamonds (pink and champagne) at several jewellers, including Costello's.

Nearby **Trinity Arcade** (www.trinityarcade.com.au) is a triple layered cake for consumers to gorge on, with treats ranging from Amorosa, an Australian ethical accessories brand and Perth's first socially conscious fashion label, to long-lost tomes in the bookshop. Hay Street, which lies at the epicentre of this retail eruption, became Australia's first pedestrian mall in 1970, and is popular with window shoppers and big spenders.

Between here and Hay Street is **Enex 100** (www.enex100.com), a contemporary urban centre where the fashion conscious can forage for threads by Australian fashion designers such as Alannah Hill. Other available labels include Guess, Dangerfield, Gorman, Decjuba and Jack London. Close by, the **Wesley Quarter** (www.wesleyquarter.com.au) offers the likes of G-Star RAW, Aquila, Oxford, Industrie, Lorna Jane, Review and Wittner.

Nearby, Euro-style **King Street Precinct** (www.kingstreetperth.com) modestly describes itself as the 'jewel

Fremantle Markets

Gold nuggets at Perth Mint

in the crown of Perth's West End', and lures with labels including Prada, Louis Vuitton, Chanel and Miu Miu.

The new kid on the shopping block is **140** (www.140.com.au), which fuses fashion with art, food and other miscellaneous funky stuff. Slightly more old school is **Forrest Chase** (www.forrestchase.com.au), where you'll find Myer Department Store and roughly 40 fashion and lifestyle stores.

MARKETS

Since 1897, **Fremantle Markets** (www.fremantlemarkets.com.au) have been pumping with produce, performers (the buskers are legendary) and peculiar must-haves, such as the surprisingly cool broad-brim hats made from recycled road train canvasses sold by Afro Blonde (www.afroblonde.com.au). There is much treasure to be explored here, in both the 'Yard' and the 'Hall', between Parry and Henderson streets.

The **Broome Courthouse Markets** (www.broomemarkets.com.au), held every Saturday all year and Sunday April–October, boast 115 creative stalls. Broome also hosts **Night Markets** (Thu, June–Sept) and **Staircase to the Moon Markets** over the two nights of the full moon during the phenomenon (Apr–Oct). Held at Town Beach Reserve on Robinson Street, the stalls sell tropical-style food and drink.

Also worth checking out are the **Town Square Markets** in Margaret River (www.townsquaremarkets.com; Sun, Nov–Apr), which sell art, crafts and handmade jewellery, and Guildford's **Stirling Square Market** (www.swanvalley.com.au; third Sun of the month), for vintage, retro and upcycled gear.

BLING

At the **Perth Mint** (www.perthmint.com) you can buy special-edition platinum, silver and gold coins. Closer to the source, Natural Gold Nuggets and Jewellery (www.naturalgoldnuggets.com.au) sells high-purity, ethically sourced minerals.

Up on the tropical Indian Ocean coast, **Willie Creek Pearl Farm** (www.williecreekpearls.com.au) offers the full immersive experience, where you can meet the oysters producing the pearls you're pondering purchasing on a helicopter tour of the aqua farm.

INDIGENOUS ART

At the **Aboriginal Art Craft Gallery** in Kings Park (www.aboriginalgallery.com.au) you can meet artists and chat about their work, some of which is available to buy. **Japingka Aboriginal Art Gallery** in Fremantle (www.japingkaaboriginalart.com) also displays and sells work by a number of astonishing artists. For more about understanding and buying indigenous art in WA, visit the Aboriginal Art Centre Hub of Western Australia (AACHWA; www.aachwa.com.au).

Live performance at Perth Concert Hall

ENTERTAINMENT

Blessed with year-round warm weather, it's no surprise that WA does its dancing under the stars. Alfresco enjoyment is the name of the entertainment game here, whether you're catching a film or watching a play or gig.

Fremantle and Perth punch above their weight in the arts and music sector, having produced some of the most exciting names on the Australian indie and rock scene in recent years, as well as a clutch of excellent actors.

MUSIC

Perth was the hometown of the Farriss brothers (Andrew, Jon and Tim), who formed the heart of INXS (behind the face of Michael Hutchinson).

More recently the city has been dubbed the 'new Seattle', after the success of local bands such as Jebediah, Eskimo Joe, Little Birdy, Gyroscope, The Sleepy Jackson, Methyl Ethel, Tame Impala, Pendulum and Knife Party.

Fremantle is where the rock band AC/DC's front man Bon Scott grew up and is buried (see page 58).

Concerts

Large live-music venues include the new **Perth Stadium** (see page 54) and the **Perth Arena** (see page 43). More intimate live experiences can be enjoyed at venues such as the **Metro** (see page 46); **Amplifier Capitol** on Murray Street (www.amplifiercapitol. com.au); **The Bird** (www.williamstreet bird.com) and **Jack Rabbit Slim's** (www.jackrabbitslims.net), both in Northbridge; and **Fly By Night** (www. flybynight.org) and **Aardvark Bar** (www. theaardvarkbar.com.au) in Fremantle.

Alfresco gigs regularly rock places such as Kings Park (see page 31), and beyond the city numerous excellent outdoor venues host bands; most notably the **Belvoir Amphitheatre** (www.belvoir.net.au/amphitheatre) and **Redhill Auditorium** (www.redhillaudito-rium.com.au).

For jazz head to **Ellington Jazz Club** in Northbridge (www.ellingtonjazz.com.au). The **Perth Concert Hall** (www.perthcon-certhall.com.au) is the main venue of the West Australian Symphony Orchestra.

PERFORMING ARTS

Oscar-winning and Golden Globe and BAFTA-nominated actor Heath Ledger (*The Dark Knight*, *Brokeback Mountain*, *A Knight's Tale*, *Two Hands*), who tragically died in 2008, was born and bred in Perth, and attended Guildford Grammar school. Sam Worthington, who grew up

A colourful fireworks display to celebrate Australia Day

in Rockingham along Perth's southern coast, shot to fame in James Cameron's *Avatar* in 2009 and *Terminator Salvation*.

The multi-award winning 2002 film *Rabbit-proof Fence* – which depicts the story of three mixed-race Aboriginal girls running away from the Moore River Native Settlement, north of Perth, to return to their families – stars Evelyn Sampi from Derby in WA, alongside Kenneth Branagh and David Gulpilil.

Theatre
Catch plays and other performances at Perth's Cultural Centre (see page 44), home to the **Blue Room Theatre** and the **State Theatre Centre**, which encompasses the Heath Ledger Theatre, Studio Underground and the Courtyard, an outdoor performance area. Also check out Subiaco's **Regal Theatre** (see page 50) and the centrally located **His Majesty's Theatre** (see page 42).

Comedy
Try the **Comedy Lounge** (413 Murray Street; www.comedylounge.com.au), the associated **Sonar Room** in Fremantle (42 Mews Road) and **Lazy Susan's Comedy Den** (292 Beaufort Street, Highgate; www.lazysusans.com.au).

Cinema
Modern multiplexes abound across Perth and WA's other towns and cities. **Cinema Paradiso** in Northbridge (164 James Street; www.palacecinemas.com.au) shows fewer blockbusters and more arthouse and foreign films.

Outdoor screenings of new films and cult classics take place throughout summer at the Moonlight Cinema in Kings Park (www.moonlight.com.au; see page 32) and Rooftop Movies in Northbridge (68 Roe Street; www.rooftopmovies.com.au).

FESTIVALS

The following is just a taste of events hosted in and around Perth.

Perth Cup (1 January; www.perthracing.org.au) A horse-racing carnival and Perth's premier fashion event.

Australia Day Skyworks (26 January) Huge display of fireworks centred around the Swan River.

Fremantle Fringe World (January–February; www.fringeworld.com.au) Comedy, circus, cabaret, music and art.

Perth Festival (February–March; www.perthfestival.com.au) The southern hemisphere's longest-established annual arts festival.

Spring in the Valley (September–October; www.springinthevalley.com.au) Celebrates people and produce of the Swan Valley with fine wines, food, art and music.

Pride Fest (October; www.pridewa.com.au) LGBTQ+ parade through the streets of Northbridge.

Fremantle Festival (November; www.fremantlefestival.com.au) Week-long celebration with street parades, parties, concerts, kites and kids' events.

Hikers on the Bibbulmun Track

ACTIVITIES

From diving amid tropical coral on Ningaloo Reef to surfing the Southern Ocean swell and hiking and biking along trails wending around the ankles of towering karri trees, WA is a place for outdoor adventure.

Western Australia retains the feel of a frontier state. You need a pioneer's pulse just to get here, but when you do, adventure opportunities surround you: wild oceans to the west and south, the tropics in the north, and the arid outback on the eastern horizon.

Activities here involve embracing the elements and exploring extraordinary landscapes amid wonderful wildlife. Most are accessible for people with average fitness and some spirit – tree-climbing in Pemberton's forests (see page 85), adventure caving on the coast (see page 85), sandboarding down Lancelin's dune mountains (see page 92) – while other challenges are best left to the experts, such as the 20km (12-mile) Rottnest Swim.

MAINSTREAM SPORTS

Of all the football codes popular in Australia, the one that really matters in WA is Aussie Rules. People are obsessed, as much with the game at a regional and community level as with the stars of the AFL (Australian Football League). Try to catch a local game. The state's two AFL teams, the West Coast Eagles and the Fremantle Dockers, both play home games at the new Perth (Optus) Stadium in East Perth, see page 54.

International cricket matches are played there too, with smaller games contested at grounds including Lilac Hill Park in Guildford. Cricket is the biggest participation team sport, with impromptu games ever igniting on beaches or in gardens and parks.

With large British, Irish, Italian and Greek communities, soccer is well supported (and widely played) too. Local A-League team Perth Glory play home games at the centrally located Perth Oval.

Tennis players can hire courts at the State Tennis Centre in East Perth (see page 55), while golfers are spoilt for choice across city and state, with both classy and quirky options available. In Lancelin you can try Fling Golf (combination of golf and lacrosse).

OUTDOOR PURSUITS

Bushwalking and trail running

The many national parks that punctuate the huge expanse of WA offer myriad bushwalking (Australian lingo for hiking) trails across an incredibly diverse land-

Sunset fishing on the beach

scape, which ranges from dry desert to deep forest. The state has several signature long-distance hiking trails including the **Bibbulmun Track** (www.bibbulmun track.org.au) between Kalamunda (Perth Hills) and Albany. Entirely in the southwest is the fantastic 125km (78-mile) Cape-to-Cape Walk (www.capetocape track.com.au) between Cape Naturaliste and Cape Leeuwin lighthouses. See **Bushwalking WA** (www.bushwalkingwa. org.au) for more.

Mountain biking
With a name that means 'path through the forest' in the Noongar language, the **Munda Biddi** (www.mundabiddi.org.au) is a world-class multi-section off-road cycling trail stretching 1000km (621 miles) through WA's Darling Range and Southern Forests, from Mundaring to Albany.

Excellent mountain-biking trails around Perth include **Goat Farm** (just off the Great Eastern Highway) and **Kalamunda Mountain** (40 minutes from the city). The southwest single track is hard to beat, though, with places like Pemberton offering trails through towering Karri trees.

Check in with the **West Australian Mountain Bike Association** (WAMBA, www.wamba.org.au) for more information.

Surfing and kitesurfing
Surfing is popular along both ocean coasts. Cottesloe and Trigg beaches are suburban Perth's best, Jake's Point in Kalbarri has a perfect left-hand break and Margaret River is a sensational big-wave spot, but there are great conditions everywhere from Esperance (excellent reef breaks) around to Geraldton (a kitesurfing hotspot).

Paddling
With its roots in the surf-lifesaving culture, ocean-/surf-ski paddling is a popular pursuit in WA, as is stand-up paddleboarding (SUP).

Diving and snorkelling
WA's Ningaloo Reef is every bit as amazing as the Great Barrier Reef, but it attracts a fraction of the crowds, and you can snorkel directly out to the coral from the beach in places like Cape Range National Park (see page 101). Snorkelling with whopping great whale sharks (Exmouth, March–August) and manta rays (Coral Bay, all year) is an utterly extraordinary experience.

Exmouth Navy Pier is regarded as one of the world's best shore dives, but there are countless dive spots around the state, including many wrecks, some close to Perth (not least around Rottnest, see page 70).

Fishing
Sea fishing is fantastic along all of WA's 20,781km (12,913-mile; including islands) coastline. Observe restrictions and no-fishing zones around marine parks. Barramundi fishing in the Kimberley is also exciting (just watch out for crocs). Charters and guides are available for both (www.fish.wa.gov.au).

Perth hosts the Empire Games, 1962

HISTORY: KEY DATES

Western Australia has been continually populated for 50 millennia. It's home to cave art that predates the pyramids by 35,000 years, created prior to the end of the last ice age, but Perth was only settled by Westerners less than 200 years ago.

BEFORE THE EUROPEANS

Circa 50,000 BC   Humans arrive in Australia from Asia via land bridges.

1290s   Marco Polo's journal refers to a land south of Java, rich in gold.

THE FIRST EUROPEANS

1606   First authenticated landing on Australian soil, by Dutchman Willem Janszoon in the *Duyfken*.

1616   Dutch explorer, Dirk Hartog, makes first authenticated landing in WA, at Shark Bay, in the *Eendracht*.

1696–7   Discovery of Swan River by Willem de Vlamingh.

1791   Discovery of King George Sound by Captain George Vancouver.

1826   King George Sound occupied by convicts.

1827   Examination of Swan River by Captain Stirling in HMS *Success*.

1828   British government approves founding of Swan River Colony.

1829   Possession of the colony is taken by Captain Fremantle; Stirling formally founds the colony.

1831   Stirling made governor; first newspaper issued.

1834   Battle of Pinjarra sees massacre of 30 Noongar people.

1846   New Norcia Mission established; discovery of coal.

1850   Convicts sent to meet labour shortage and help build Perth.

1856   Queen Victoria grants Perth city status.

1868   Convict transportation ends.

1870   Colony gains representative government.

1877   Telegraph links Perth and London.

1881   Eastern railway links Perth, Fremantle and Guildford.

1885   Gold found at Halls Creek.

STATEHOOD

1890   Sir John Forrest forms WA's first government.

1892   Construction of Fremantle Harbour begins.

America's Cup, 1987

Australian Prime Minister Scott Morrison

1893 Paddy Hannan's Kalgoorlie find becomes 'The Golden Mile'.

1899 Women get the vote, ahead of Britain, Canada and the US; 1,231 WA men fight in the Boer War.

1900 WA votes 'yes' in federal referendum.

1901 Commonwealth of Australia inaugurated 1 January; WA becomes a state of federal Australia.

WAR AND PEACE

1914–18 6,000 Western Australians die in World War I.

1915 Anzac fleet assembles in King George Sound for the assault on Gallipoli, Turkey. WA's 10th Light Horse Regiment prominent.

1917 Trans-Australian Railway links WA to eastern states.

1929 Fremantle becomes a city.

1933 WA votes to opt out of federation, but the UK government rules the move unconstitutional.

1939–45 Perth men and women serve in World War II.

1950s The Causeway and Narrows Bridge span the Swan.

1952 Britain explodes atomic bombs on the Monte Bello islands. Two more explode in 1956.

1962 Perth hosts Empire Games.

1983 Labor begins 10-year period of government in WA.

1987 America's Cup held in Fremantle.

1993 WA Liberal/National coalition ousts Labor.

1999 World's earliest known lifeform, 3.5 billion-year-old stromatolites, found in WA outback.

21ST CENTURY

2006 WA resources boom begins.

2007 Labor Party, under Kevin Rudd, wins landslide national election victory.

2008 Colin Barnett (Liberal Party) becomes WA Premier for two terms.

2010 Kevin Rudd replaced by Australia's first female Prime Minister, Julia Gillard, until 2013, when Rudd regains leadership.

2013 Tony Abbot leads Liberal Party to win national election.

2015 Malcolm Turnbull replaces Tony Abbott as Liberal Party leader and Prime Minister, and defeats Labor party by a single seat in the 2016 election.

2016 Elizabeth Quay opens, with work continuing.

2017 Mark McGowan (Labor) becomes WA Premier.

2018 Scott Morrison replaces Malcolm Turnbull as Liberal Party leader and Prime Minister; Yagan Square and Perth Stadium open.

2019–20 FOMO, a $220-million project to redevelop Fremantle city centre, continues.

BEST ROUTES

1. Swan River and Kings Park   30
2. Perth Water and South Bank   34
3. City Centre and Old Perth   38
4. Cultural Centre and
      Northbridge   44
5. Subiaco   48
6. East Perth   52
7. Fremantle   56
8. Perth's suburban beaches   62
9. Rottnest   68
10. Swan Valley   72
11. South of Perth   78
12. Margaret River and
       Southwest   82
13. Southern Ocean and
       Goldfields   88
14. North of Perth to Shark Bay   92
15. Ningaloo and the Pilbara   98
16. Broome and the Kimberley   103

SWAN RIVER AND KINGS PARK

Perth straddles the wide, beautiful mouth of the Swan River, a feature that defines the city and is best appreciated from Kings Park, with its splendid panoramic views across Melville Water and Matilda Bay.

DISTANCE: 9km (5.5 miles)
TIME: A half day
START: Swan Bells
END: The Landing
POINTS TO NOTE: The exciting precinct of Elizabeth Quay will continue to evolve. This route is possible in a morning or afternoon, but you can easily lose an entire day exploring Kings Park and the Botanic Gardens. This route can be combined with others including Route 2.

It can come as a surprise to first-time visitors that Perth isn't perched right on the Indian Ocean, but is instead 14km (9 miles) upstream from the port of Fremantle. Some of Australia's most sensational suburban beaches are nearby, but the city itself is synonymous with a serpentine stretch of fresh water, the Swan River.

Overlooking this, on a hill ambitiously called Mount Eliza, is the semi-wild suburban bushland of Kings Park, over 400 hectares (990 acres) of leafy seclusion.

ELIZABETH QUAY AND BARRACK SQUARE

Opened in 2016, the Elizabeth Quay development has completely transformed the CBD side of the riverfront, with Esplanade Reserve flooded by an artificial inlet with jetties and an island, which is linked to Riverside Drive to the west by a stunning bridge for pedestrians and cyclists. The quay is surrounded by ultra-modern hotels, recreation and play areas, public art, and retail and living space.

The bells

Start at the **Swan Bells** (Barrack Square, Riverside Drive; tel: 08-6210 0444; www.thebelltower.com.au; daily from 10am), where immense copper sails cup a green-glass belltower. The bells were installed to mark Australia's bicentenary in 1988. Inside the tower you can see the bells, take part in an interactive bell-chiming demonstration and visit the outside observation level, with views across Perth and the river.

Barrack Street Jetty remains the departure point for various boat cruises

to Fremantle and Rottnest Island, and up to the wineries in the Swan Valley (see page 72), although the ferry to South Perth now leaves from Elizabeth Quay.

Bridge over water

Head west, through shiny **Elizabeth Quay ❶** (www.mra.wa.gov.au), perusing the walkways, retail outlets and restaurants such as **The Reveley** (see ❶). Cross the **Elizabeth Quay Bridge**, a 20-metre (66ft) -high suspended cycle- and walkway that has quickly become iconic, to William Street Landing.

Pass the **First Contact** sculpture, a gleaming 5-metre (16ft) -tall aluminum artwork by indigenous artist Laurel Nan-

nup, which depicts the arrival of European settlers.

Follow the curve of the Swan, along the shared path (bikes and pedestrians) that runs parallel to Riverside Drive. Pass through David Carr Memorial Park, go under the Mitchell Freeway and cross Mounts Bay Road to enter Kings Park by the Kennedy Fountain, ascending the steep Kokoda Memorial Track to meet Hacketts Path.

KINGS PARK AND BOTANIC GARDENS

This area of urban bushland is wrapped around the flanks of Mount Eliza (more hill than mountain), known as Kaarta Gar-up or Mooro Katta by the Noongar. The manicured lawns, terraces and

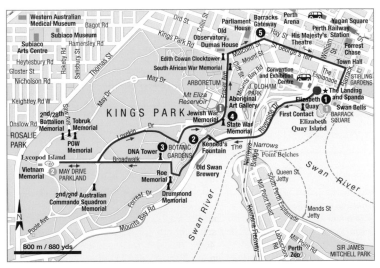

water gardens are substantial, but most of this extraordinary park is dominated by native bush, which makes it unique.

Park Visitor Information (Fraser Avenue; www.bgpa.wa.gov.au; daily 9.30am–4pm) offers free bush and wildflower walks, leaving daily from Fraser Avenue, outside Aspects of Kings Park. **Segway Tours** are also available (www.segwaytourswa.com.au), and bikes can be hired from **Spinway WA** (Fraser Avenue; tel: 0413 343 305; www.spinwaywa.bike).

Skywalking

Go east on Hacketts Path for about 100 metres/yds before turning right to meet the **Lotterywest Federation Walkway** – a 620-metre/yd-long hovering path, suspended amid a canopy of tall eucalypts, with great vistas over the Swan – leading right into the **Botanic Gardens ②**. You will find yourself in a forest of exotic plants and trees here, including many hundreds of native species.

Just west of the **Water Garden Pavilion**, cross Forest Drive and head to the **DNA Tower ③**, so called because of its twin-helix circular staircases, each with 101 steps leading to a platform with views across the park and out to Rottnest Island (see page 68).

Chasing dinosaurs

To see more of the park, follow the Honeyeater Path along the **Broadwalk** for just over 1.5km (1 mile) to reach a lake and **Lycopod Island**, complete with play-ground, model dinosaurs, timber-and-steel lycopods (the world's first trees), and calamites (fern-like plants).

In a steel cage nearby is a growing 'dinosaur tree', a **Wollemi Pine**, thought to have been extinct until the 1990s, when a grove of them was discovered in a secret gorge in Wollemi National Park, New South Wales. You can also view the **Vietnam Memorial** or, after dusk, enjoy an alfresco film experience at **Perth's Moonlight Cinema** (www.moonlight.com.au). Also here is **Zamia Café** (see ②).

Head southwest along Lovekin Drive to see more military memorials en route to the **University of Western Australia** (www.uwa.edu.au), where numerous impressive features include the Sunken Garden, the Reflection Pool, and the *Five Lamps of Learning*, a Venetian glass-tile mosaic by the Victorian artist Walter Napier.

War and peace

Our walk, however, returns east along Lovekin to the busiest part of the park, via the **Pioneer Women's Memorial**. Both Lovekin and May drives are lined with gums commemorating the fallen of two world wars, and just beyond the roundabout where they converge, is the solemn **State War Memorial ④**.

Approached along the Ceremonial Walk you will pass through the Court of Contemplation, past the Flame of Remembrance and Pool of Reflection, before reaching the **Cenotaph** itself,

The Glass Arched Bridge runs from Kings Park into the Botanic Garden

which is the best place in the city to get an eyeful of the Swan River delta and a panoramic vista of Perth's metropolitan area.

Fraser Avenue
Nearby you'll find a choice of eateries with river views.

Opposite, on the riverside of Fraser Avenue, is the **Aboriginal Art Gallery** (www.aboriginalgallery.com.au; Mon–Fri 10.30am–4.30pm, Sat–Sun 11am–4pm). This appropriately placed gallery sells fine indigenous arts and crafts. It usually has an indigenous artist in residence.

Follow Fraser Avenue north, passing beneath magnificent lemon-scented gums (locally known as widow-makers because of their habit of shedding large branches during times of drought), which were planted to mark Queen Victoria's Jubilee in 1898, and then added to for WA's 1929 centenary.

Back to barrack
Leave the park via the gate by the **Edith Cowan Clocktower**, and carefully cross Malcolm Street. Opposite is the **Old Perth Observatory** (www.nationaltrust.org.au), built in 1896–1900 and originally charged with watching out for bush fires in Kings Park.

Turn right, walk along Malcolm Street, crossing over the freeway, from where you can see the **Parliament of Western Australia** (tel: 08-9222 7222; www.parliament.wa.gov.au; tours Mon & Thu 10.30am, Fri 2pm) to your left.

Ahead is the **Barracks Gateway** ❺, the remains of the Pensioners' Barracks, which once housed the Enrolled Pensioner Force, made up of British soldiers who arrived as convict guards. The barracks were demolished to make way for the Mitchell Freeway.

Landing zone
Continue into St George's Terrace and the heart of Old Perth (see page 39). Follow this to Barrack Street, then go right and return to Elizabeth Quay.

After entering the quay from the north, veer right to explore **The Landing**, the precinct's primary public event space.

Food and drink

❶ THE REVELEY
Eastern Promenade, Elizabeth Quay; tel: 08-6314 1350; www.thereveleybar.com.au; daily 11am–late; $$$
The ground floor here is the perfect place to grab a coffee to start your day. Return for an evening meal in the dining room or on Henry's rooftop – seafood is the go-to.

❷ ZAMIA CAFÉ
50 May Drive, Kings Park; tel: 08-9388 6700; www.zamiacafe.com.au; daily 8am–4.30pm, later at weekends; $$$
Sensationally situated café serving breakfasts (smoked salmon, peace eggs), lunches (lemon pepper squid, slow roasts), coffees and cakes for eating in or out.

Kangaroos on Heirisson Island

PERTH WATER AND SOUTH BANK

Between Heirisson Island and the Narrows, the throat of the Swan swells into Perth Water, a wide expanse of shimmering blue water lined by footpaths and green parks, perfect for a wander with the cityscape of WA's capital as a backdrop.

DISTANCE: 7km (4.5 miles)
TIME: A half day
START: Signature Ring
END: Mends Street Jetty, South Perth
POINTS TO NOTE: This route can be done as a circular escapade, with the footpath over the Narrows Bridge closing the loop and returning you to Riverside Drive on the north bank. However, it's a much more enjoyable experience to combine the main part of the walk with a ferry ride back to Elizabeth Quay from Mends Street Jetty.

East of the Elizabeth Quay, beyond the clutch of the Narrows, the Swan spreads its wonderful wings. Central to the city's foundation (capital of what was originally called the Swan River Colony) and integral to the culture of the modern metropolis, this waterway flows through Perth in a gracious curve befitting its name, forming a riparian recreation zone where locals and visitors walk, talk, run, ride, row, eat, sip or just sit, gazing across the ripples.

This route, around Perth Water, explores both banks, taking intrepid urban adventurers via the island home of a small mob of semi-wild kangaroos, and delivering a view back across the city to Mount Eliza.

TIME RING

Start at the **Signature Ring** on Barrack Street Jetty. This installation, a collaborative effort by local artists Simon Gauntlett and Matthew Ngui, is shaped like giant headphones, threaded with fibre optics that illuminate movement on interactive panels – great fun to mess around with, quite dramatic after dark, and symbolic of the passage of time. It also features hundreds of thousands of school students' signatures etched in copper plates, which were collected in 1999 as part of the millennium celebrations.

ALONG THE SWAN

Head east along the palm-fringed footpath that traces Riverside Drive,

Statue of Yagan on Heirisson Island

passing the restored clapboard boat-house of the **Western Australia Rowing Club ❶**, founded in 1868, a beautiful building jutting into the river, shared by an amazing coffee-roasting café, **Rubra on the Swan** (see ❶). Langley Park, to the left, was Perth's first airfield. It is used for special events, and various circuses pitch their big tops here.

The path hops across a series of boardwalks at **Point Fraser ❷**, near the foot of the Causeway, where there are picnic and barbecue facilities, plus a children's playground, amid examples of indigenous flora. Once a wetlands reserve, this prime piece of land has recently been redeveloped, with a function centre, a restaurant – the **Point Bar and Grill** (see ❷) – and, in summer, a pop-up alfresco watering hole called **Embargo On the Point**

(www.embargo.com.au), all of which take advantage of the killer Swan River views.

ISLAND HOPPING

At the end of Riverside Drive, follow the path onto the Causeway and cross to **Heirisson Island ❸**. Turn right off the Causeway, with the river on your right follow the track down towards an orange sign. A small colony of western grey kangaroos are housed in an enclosure here, bringing an iconic bush element right into the city. During the heat of the day the kangaroos stay under cover, but if you move quietly around the track there's a good chance of finding them grazing. Rangers feed them in the cooler, early evenings.

A 2km (1-mile) track runs around Heirisson Island. At the southern tip is a bronze statue of **Yagan**, a Noongar warrior. Yagan was the son of Beeliar tribal chief Midgegooroo. He became an outlaw after he and his father were accused of spearing to death two white labourers at Maddington Farm, near Fremantle. Midgegooroo was caught and executed by firing squad at Perth's original jail (now part of the **Deanery**

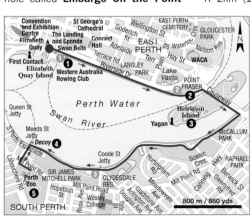

Tasmanian devil at Perth Zoo

on St George's Terrace, see page 39), but Yagan remained free for months, until a £30 reward proved too tempting for the teenage Keates brothers, who feigned friendship and then shot him dead.

Yagan's head – removed after he was killed in 1833 so a bounty could be claimed, and subsequently taken to the UK to be exhibited as an anthropological curiosity – was retrieved by tribal elders in 1997 and was finally buried during a traditional ceremony in the Swan Valley in 2010.

The island was named after a French sailor, Midshipman François Heirisson. Long before the founding of Perth, he rowed a longboat all the way upriver to the island from his moored ship Le Naturaliste, which carried Nicolas Baudin's scientific expedition of 1801–4.

As late as the 1920s, squatters lived rough in shacks on the island, in sight of Government House. Several times in more recent years (2012, 2015 and 2016) refugee camps were established here, and an attempt was made to set up a Tent Embassy like the one in Canberra, in response to the withdrawal of land rights in WA and the shutting down of indigenous communities.

THE SOUTH BANK

On the southern side of the Causeway riverside parkland leads downriver, with a café, boat ramp and boat hire at Coode Street. Also here is the popular restaurant, **The Boatshed** (see ③).

At **Mends Street Jetty** the Transperth Ferry (www.transperth.wa.gov.au) departs

---

Perth Zoo

When the city zoo opened in 1897, six keepers looked after an orangutan, two monkeys, four ostriches, a pair of lions and a tiger. Now there are over 1,400 animals from 169 species, and around 120 staff.

Originally the zoo was a place of entertainment and leisure, with natural hot springs, tea rooms, ornamental gardens, 'beautiful baby' contests and tennis matches. In 1909 the zoo even hosted the Australasian Open. Today the accent is on animal conservation and education, and in 2017 the zoo released its 4,000th animal back into the wild. Beautiful baby contests are a thing of the past, but there are still evening concerts, special events and activities for kids.

One of the highlights is the Australian Bushwalk through recreations of different Australian ecosystems, from the arid interior to a tropical rainforest. In an Australian wetlands exhibit, boardwalks wind through a huge aviary and pool complex, with a thrilling array of water birds and freshwater crocodiles. Sadly, the zoo's popular estuarine crocodile, 5-metre (16ft) long Simmo, passed away in 2018.

The Boatshed offers great views

for Elizabeth Quay every 15 minutes at busy times, and runs into evening (check website for last sailing). Also moored at Mends Street is the paddle steamer, **Decoy** ❹ (www.psdecoy.com.au), which embarks on various cruises, often involving live music. A genuine steam-powered ferry, it has plied the river for many years as a pleasure craft.

Mends Street has a multitude of eating options. Restaurants facing the river are especially popular at night when the illuminated skyline of the Perth CBD is enchanting.

If you're feeling very energetic, the cycle/pedestrian pathway runs on from Mends Street, under the Narrows, all the way to Fremantle. To return to the north bank, catch a ferry, or cross the bridge. But first you might like to visit **Perth Zoo** ❺ (see box) (20 Labouchere Road, South Perth; tel: 08-9474 4420; www.perthzoo.wa.gov.au; daily 9am–5pm), a five-minute walk from Mends Street.

Food and drink

❶ RUBRA ON THE SWAN

171 Riverside Drive; tel: 08-6555 1844; www.rubraontheswan.com.au; daily 6am–2pm; $$

Sharing a stunning boathouse with the Western Australian Rowing Club, this award-winning coffee-roasting café is a cracking spot for a caffeinated kick-start, or some breakfast (try the smashed avocado) or lunch (ace burgers) before you start exploring.

❷ POINT BAR AND GRILL

306 Riverside Drive, East Perth; tel: 08-9218 8088; www.thepointbarandgrill.com.au; Mon–Thu noon–late, Fri–Sun from 11am; $$

Sitting pretty on the banks of the Swan River at Point Fraser, this rooftop restaurant, bar and grill is thrilling Swansiders and visitors with its modern, unpretentious Australian menu. During popular Sunday sunset sessions you can score a slow-cooked chook, salad and chips with a glass of chardonnay, all for $25, including the wine. There's a wide selection of craft ales, cocktails and quality wines to sample. Expect live music at weekends.

❸ THE BOATSHED

Coode Street Jetty, South Perth; tel: 08-9474 1314; www.boatshedrestaurant.com; Mon–Sat 8am–late, Sun 8am–4pm; $$$

From its position on the south bank of the Swan, the Boatshed offers 180-degree views of Perth City, Kings Park and the river itself. The food – Australian ingredients with a large sprig of international inspiration – lives up to the vista too. Try the Sichuan pepper calamari with Thai slaw, or Cone Bay barramundi with sweet potato puree. Breakfast and café menus are also available.

The Bell Tower

CITY CENTRE AND OLD PERTH

Perth's busy CBD is growing up fast, with an expanding crowd of cloud tickling skyscrapers, visible from all around the city and far beyond. Less apparent are the Victorian buildings in their shadow, remnants of Perth's earliest days.

DISTANCE: 4.5km (3 miles)
TIME: A half day
START: Swan Belltower
END: Yagan Square
POINTS TO NOTE: Take a break from pounding the pavements during this route by enjoying the grassy gardens and the culture-rich recreational breathing space that is Yagan Square, named after an indigenous warrior.

As the nucleus of the Swan River Colony in 1829, Perth started small and only began to swell with the arrival of convicts in the 1850s, by which time it was the capital of what was being called Western Australia. The oldest buildings here were built by convict labour, but it was the 1890s gold-rush wealth that transformed Perth into a city proper paying for hundreds of public buildings.

The city now glistens with glass-and-steel towers, entertainment and leisure centres cluster along the riverbanks, and revitalised public buildings and cultural centres occupy former industrial sites.

Completed only recently, the Perth City Link scheme has submerged the bus station and railway line that once dissected the city, reconnecting Northbridge to the urban centre, and creating public plazas like Yagan Square.

STIRLING GARDENS

Many historic buildings disappeared in the 20th-century redevelopment, but those that remain are elegant reminders of times before the streets were paved with gold – or even tarmac. The best place to take in Perth's architectural heritage is St George's Terrace, Perth's first thoroughfare, stretching the length of the CBD (Central Business District).

Start at the Bell Tower and walk north along Barrack Street. The grassy expanse of the **Supreme Court Gardens** are on the right.

Around here, and in the adjacent **Stirling Gardens ❶**, the first settlers pitched their tents in 1829. A collection of surviving structures date back almost to Perth's birth. Treasured residents of the gardens include a massive Moreton Bay

Gumnut Babies at Stirling Gardens

The Deanery

fig tree, and a pair of Gumnut Babies, Snugglepot and Cuddlepie – sculptures of two characters created by Australia author May Gibbs (Cuddlepie was stolen in 2015, but replaced 18 months later).

Perth's first brick building was the **Old Court House** (1836), which shares the gardens with the **Supreme Court of Western Australia** (1903; www. supremecourt.wa.gov.au), some parts of which are publicly accessible.

Opposite is **Council House**, the modern headquarters of Perth City Council, and **Government House**, residence of the state governor.

ST GEORGE'S TERRACE

Rejoin Barrack Street and continue to the junction with St George's Terrace, then turn right. Outside **Council House** (a building straight from the 1960s, creatively lit by LEDs after dark) you'll encounter a larger than life-size mob of bouncing bronze kangaroos, a much-photographed feature of the city centre since they were installed in 1998.

Opposite is **St George's Cathedral ❷** (www.perthcathedral.org; daily 7am–6pm), constructed 1879–88 by convicts from hand-made bricks. It was completed four years before the WA gold rush, when Perth's citizens couldn't even afford a spire, but a square tower was added in 1902, as a memorial to Queen Victoria.

The bold, billowing white sculpture standing on the corner of St George's Terrace and Cathedral Avenue is an abstract interpretation of the legend of St George and the dragon, representing the triumph of good over evil, created in 2011 by artists Marcus Canning and Christian de Vietri.

Next door to St George's Cathedral is **The Deanery ❸**, built in 1859 as a residence for the first Dean of St George's Cathedral, George Purvis Pownall. Prior to this, the site housed Perth's original jail, where mostly indigenous prisoners were held and Yagan's father Midgegooroo was executed by firing squad, without trial, in 1833 (see page 35).

On the opposite corner of Pier Street, right by heritage-listed St Andrew's Church, a 62-storey, 222-metre (730ft) golden skyscraper is planned, which will change Perth's profile once again.

Back on the other side of the road is **Perth Concert Hall** (www.perthconce

Colourfully lit Council House

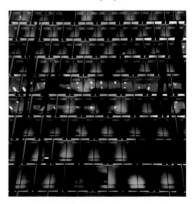

Perth Concert Hall

rthall.com.au), a superb auditorium and home to the West Australian Symphony Orchestra.

Next to the concert hall, at No. 1 St George's Terrace, is **The Duxton**, Perth's tax office until its transformation into one of the city's best hotels in 1996. East of here is Adelaide Terrace, the location of more hotels. In the early days of the colony houses backed onto the water here and people swam from their gardens.

Gold route

Turn left along Hill Street and stop for a sensational caffeine hit at **DuoTone** (see ❶), beside the **Perth Mint ❹** (310 Hay Street; tel: 08-9421 7428; www. perthmint.com; daily 9am–5pm). This started life in 1899 as a branch of the Royal Mint, London, and has the look of a colonial mansion – with two wings, central riser and flagpole. The elegant front lawns feature a statue of prospectors cast in bronze. Australia's oldest working mint, it's always busy producing special editions.

Inside, you can experience a reconstructed turn-of-the-century miners' camp, get your hands on a 400-ounce gold bar and watch a gold pour. The guided tour (hourly 9.30am–3.30pm) takes you through the Gold Exhibition and finishes in time to see the molten gold poured into ingots. You can conclude a visit with a Devonshire cream tea in the period restaurant.

Head west along Goderich Street to Victoria Square, dominated by the catho-

lic **St Mary's Cathedral** (www.stmarys cathedralperth.com.au; open daily; tours Tue 10.30am). On the southeast side of the square is Mercedes College, a Catholic School originally founded in

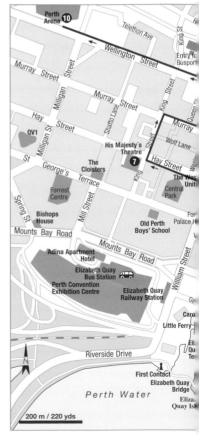

St Mary's Cathedral

Royal Perth Hospital

1846 by Irish Sisters of Mercy. On the opposite corner of the square is the **Royal Perth Hospital**, which started life as a medical tent pitched on the site in June 1830.

Leave Victoria Square on Murray Street and pass beneath the boughs of a magnificent Morton Bay fig, which spans the road. Just past the tree, on the left, you'll find the **Old Perth Fire Station**,

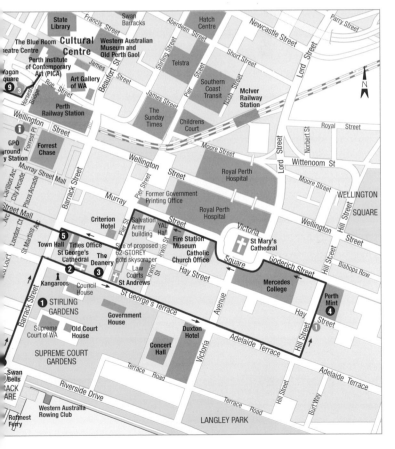

Hay Street Mall

which dates to around 1900 and contains a heritage centre and museum.

Time travel

A parade of intact historic buildings follows, including the headquarters of the **Young Australia League** (YAL) and a beautiful **Salvation Army** building.

Duck left along Pier Street and then turn right to walk along Hay Street, passing the Art Deco **Criterion Hotel**. On the corner of Cathedral Avenue is the **Titles Office** (1897), considered the best work of George Temple Poole who, as colonial architect in the gold rush, turned out 300 public buildings in just two years (1895–97).

On the corner with Barrack Street is the stunning red-brick **Town Hall** ❺ (tel: 08-9229 2965; www.visitperth.com.au; Mon–Sat 10am–4pm, tours Thu 2pm), built by convicts between 1867–70 using local materials like jarrah and sheoak, Swan Valley limestone and clay bricks from the east Perth quarry – later Queens Gardens.

TOP SHOPPING

Cross Barrack Street into popular **Hay Street Mall**, Australia's first pedestrianised mall and a good place to grab a bite (try **Jaws**, see ❷).

Further west, the **Wesley Quarter** ❻ (www.wesleyquarter.com.au) lures serious label-lovers with boutiques by Australian fashion designers such as Alannah Hill and shops offering the likes of G-Star RAW, Aquila, Oxford, Industrie, Lorna Jane, Review and Wittner.

At the crossroads formed by Hay and King streets, you will find one of Perth's finest buildings, the Edwardian Baroque beauty that is **His Majesty's Theatre** ❼ (www.ptt.wa.gov.au).

Turn right and wander through the **King Street Precinct** (www.kingstreet perth.com), which aims to recreate a European-accented shopping experience with restored buildings and high-end brand-orientated outlets.

Take a right into Murray Street and then go left on William Street to discover the newest addition to Perth's consumerscape: **140** ❽ (www.140.com.au), an urban space that blends trendy shops, tasty eating and watering holes, and contemporary street art. On the other side of the block, opposite the old General Post Office building, is **Forrest Chase** (www.forrestchase.com.au), home to Myer Department Store, and around 40 fashion and lifestyle stores.

Yagan Square

Part of the major new Perth City Link development project, **Yagan Square** ❾ is a large communal art and leisure space, situated between Horseshoe Bridge and the now-submerged Perth Busport.

Named after a Noongar warrior who resisted British settlement (see page 35 for Yagan's story), the square's design contains multiple cultural references to the indigenous people on whose land it stands, and pays trib-

Yagan Square

ute to the lakes that once existed here before Perth railway station and Wellington Street were built.

Besides boasting a children's play area, market hall, eateries (**Toast my Curry**, see ③, is amazing), gardens, water features and an amphitheatre, it features art installations including a 45-metre (148ft) -high digital tower with a 30-metre by 14-metre (100ft by 45ft) wrap-around display screen, and 14 columns erupting from its midst – one for each of the Noongar language groups. Looking towards William Street, is *Wirin*, a statue designed by Noongar artist Tjyllyungoo and representing the 'sacred force of creative power that connects all life of *boodja* (mother earth)'.

Perth Arena

Just north, on the other side of the Horseshoe Bridge lies Perth's Cultural Centre and the nightlife-rich suburb of Northbridge (see page 46), but the city's newest entertainment venue stands just 500 metres/yds west of here, along Wellington Street.

With a design based on the Eternity Puzzle, ultramodern **Perth Arena** ⑩ (www.racarena.com.au) was opened in late 2012, as part of the Perth City Link redevelopment project. With a capacity of up to 15,000 it hosts basketball, netball and tennis games, plus live music events and gigs.

Food and drink

① DUOTONE

313 Hay Street; tel: 08-9325 9396; www.duo-tone.com.au; 6.30am–3pm; $$

A top spot for a quality coffee or a little treat to keep your feet going for the rest of the route. Healthy breakfasts (vegan options available) and brilliant brews are a speciality – try the veggie shakshuka for a flavour-onslaught.

② JAWS

Shop 1, 726 Hay Street Mall; tel: 08-9481 1445; www.jawssushi.com.au; Mon–Thu 11.30am–6pm, Fri 11.30am–9pm, Sat–Sun 11.30–5.30pm; $$

The perfect place for a quick, super tasty lunch in the midst of a shopping mission, this sensational sushi train chain also has stations at other locations. Happy hour, when bargain bites can be snapped up, is Monday–Thursday 3pm–6pm.

③ TOAST MY CURRY

Yagan Square; tel: 0450 061 808; www.facebook.com/ToastMyCurry; 11am–8pm; $

Street food flavours straight from Mumbai, served in toasted naan bread. The spicy toasties (NAASTIES) come with traditional curry condiments like mango chutney and are accompanied by samosas and salads. A percentage of the profits goes towards educating and feeding slum children in India.

The Urban Orchard community garden

CULTURAL CENTRE AND NORTHBRIDGE

Cosmopolitan, cool and, until recently, aloof from the city, Northbridge has a subculture all of its own. Renowned for its nightlife and European ambience, recent developments have brought both this suburb and the Cultural Centre closer to Perth's heart.

DISTANCE: 3km (2 miles)
TIME: A half day
START: Yagan Square
END: William Street
POINTS TO NOTE: While this walk can easily be done in an hour, the museums and galleries in the Cultural Centre alone could easily take up several days of your time.

From sweaty swamp to secluded suburb and then swinging nightspot, Northbridge has been on quite the journey over the last two centuries. In recent decades it has become known for after-dark venues, a thriving latte culture and an enforced detachment from the rest of the city, due to being on the wrong side of the tracks, quite literally.

But bohemian Northbridge – and the Cultural Centre that borders it – are no longer separated from the CBD by crude infrastructure, not since the Perth City Link project sent both the Fremantle railway line and Wellington Street Bus Station underground, and Yagan Square (see page 42) was built over the freshly healed scar.

CULTURAL CENTRE

Start in **Yagan Square** (see page 42) – between the now-subterranean Perth Busport and the city railway station. Exit the square to the east, onto Horseshoe Bridge, carefully cross the road and take the walkway via the **Urban Orchard ❶** (a rooftop oasis and meeting spot, complete with communal vegetable plots and fruit trees) into Perth's culture hub, which is not officially within Northbridge, but is a fitting neighbour.

Art trail

The **Art Gallery of Western Australia ❷** (www.artgallery.wa.gov.au; Wed–Mon 10am–5pm) is the main building to the right after you cross into the centre, its slab-sided face generally advertising the latest exhibition. Inside, several floors of modern, well-lit galleries display more than 1,000 works of art, including Australian and international paintings, sculpture, prints, crafts and decorative arts.

State Library of Western Australia

Ancient history

Across a pedestrianised section of James Street is the **Western Australian Museum** ❸ (www.museum.wa.gov.au; daily 9.30am–5pm) an elegant red-brick and sandstone building with a colonnaded upper floor. In WA, scientists have access to some of Earth's oldest rocks and life forms, and a wealth of early man artefacts, including the Pilbara rock paintings.

In 1999, a fossil proving the earliest evidence of life on earth was discovered in WA's Pilbara region. Now on display in the Dinosaur Gallery, it looks like a slab of red rock, but it holds stromatolites estimated to be 3.5 billion years old. Living versions still grow in the highly saline water of Hamelin Pool at Shark Bay (see page 97).

The museum has a pleasant coffee shop next to the **Old Gaol**, which was built by convicts in 1855–6 and is now crammed with memorabilia of Perth life since James Stirling's 1827 expedition.

Books and drama

Next door is the **State Library** ❹ (www.slwa.wa.gov.au; Mon–Thu 9am–8pm, Fri 9am–5.30pm, Sat–Sun 10am–5.30pm), where one wing is occupied by the **Battye Library of Western Australian History**, which contains state film and photographs. In front of the library, Akio Makigawa's black-and-white sculpture *Coalesce*

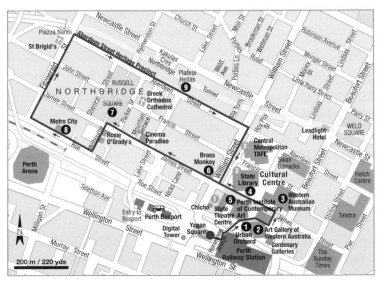

Brass Monkey Hotel

(its stepped form symbolises the stages of acquiring knowledge) has become a popular meeting place.

WA's creative arts scene revolves around the Northbridge end of the Cultural Centre, location of the **Perth Institute of Contemporary Art ❺** (PICA; James Street, Northbridge; www.pica. org.au; Mon–Fri 10am–6pm, gallery Tue–Sun 11am–6pm), the **Blue Room Theatre** (53 James Street, Northbridge; www.blueroom.org.au), and the **State Theatre Centre** (174–176 William Street; www.ptt.wa.gov.au), home to the **Heath Ledger Theatre**, named in honour of the late Perth-born actor.

NORTHBRIDGE

Leaving the Cultural Centre, cross William Street by the beautiful Great Western Hotel building (built 1896) with its distinctive verandas, now rather rowdily occupied by the **Brass Monkey ❻**, a social mix-use space to eat, drink, host functions, watch sports and more.

Euro vision

On sleepy sunny days and long summer evenings, a Mediterranean atmosphere prevails in this area; the streets are ideal for early evening strolling, alfresco dining, dawdling and people watching.

The junction of William and James streets, the hub of the entertainment district, is a good place to sit over a coffee or bottle of wine and take Northbridge's pulse. Lunch options include the excellent **Bivouac** (see ❶), ideally followed by a sensational gelato from nearby **Chichos**, where the flavours include jalapeno pineapple and green tea with caramelised white chocolate.

Gelato in hand, wander west along James Street and pass beneath the funky *Arch* artwork that straddles the roundabout at the junction with Lake Street. Continue west, past **Cinema Paradiso** (www. palacecinemas.com.au), where you can take in arthouse and international flicks in several classy European style theatres.

Park life

Opposite Rosie O'Grady's pub is **Russell Square ❼**, known to the Italian community as Parco dei Sospire ('The Park of Sighs'). Rejuvenated in the 1990s, the grassy, tree-lined square is home to a bandstand, where concerts are regularly held, and 30 sculptures by local artists Greg James and Drago Dadich.

The cast-iron artworks represent WA's development and Northbridge's diversity: the granite galleon symbolises European influence, the pagoda the Asian community's impact on the area, the bronze snake and bearded dragon reflect the natural environment, a child's school bag hints of hope for the future, while fun and entertainment are represented by a bush hat, towel and sunglasses.

Plays and plazas

Duck left along Milligan Street and turn right on Roe Street to walk by **Metro City ❽** (146 Roe Street; tel: 08-9228

Perth Arena   *The Hummus Club*

0500; www.metroconcertclub.com), a buzzing culture and entertainment venue that stages everything from art exhibitions to theatre, DJs and live gigs – much edgier content than the Perth Arena opposite (see page 43).

Turn right on Fitzgerald Street, which leads to St Brigid's Church and the **Piazza Nanni**, named after one of St Brigid's long-serving parish priests.

Opposite is the start of the **Aberdeen Street Heritage Precinct**, celebrating one of Perth's best-preserved streets, with colourful houses and shops in a range of architectural styles, some dating back to the gold rush era. A couple of blocks down, off to the left along Lake Street, is **Plateia Hellas** ❾ and the *Nexus* stone-and-water artwork formed from seven ribbed terrazzo columns, polished concrete pillars based on classical Greek architecture, interspersed with seven illuminated water jets. The square, which is especially attractive at night, was completed in 2003 to celebrate Northbridge's Greek community.

At William Street, turn right and walk back towards your starting point, perusing the many tempting refreshment options, including the **Hummus Club** (see ❷) and the magic little speakeasy, the **Mechanic's Institute** (see ❸).

Food and drink

❶ BIVOUAC CANTEEN & BAR
198 William Street; tel: 08-9227 0883; www.bivouac.com.au; Tue–Sat noon–late; $$$
A super tasty Eastern influenced and Mediterranean menu awaits at this uber cool William Street favourite, run by palette provocateurs who travel the world in search of new recipes and flavours, but source their ingredients locally. The restaurant is also a gallery, with the work of local artists showcased on the walls.

❷ HUMMUS CLUB
258 William Street; tel: 08-9227 8215; www.thehummusclub.com; Tue–Sat noon–10pm, Sun 5–10pm; $$

Sensational Lebanese and Middle Eastern cuisine is on offer here, in relaxed and non-pretentious surrounds. Apart from the signature hummus, get stuck into the Zaatar fried chicken or spiced beef, and finish the experience off with a baklava ice cream sandwich.

❸ MECHANIC'S INSTITUTE
Rear of 222 William Street; tel: 08-9228 4189; www.mechanicsinstitutebar.com.au; daily noon–midnight; $$
Tucked back from the main thoroughfare of William's Street, and a million miles away from the boorish Brass Monkey opposite, this classy boutique bar is named after the establishments that were set up in the 1800s to provide life-changing education to the working class. Expect brilliant beers and burgers.

SUBIACO

Stylish Subiaco has long been regarded as Perth's chic corner, home to the coolest start-ups, the best-dressed party-ready people and the trendiest boutiques, bars and restaurants. Rapacious developers have robbed the suburb of some soul recently, but Subiaco still swaggers.

DISTANCE: 3km (2 miles)
TIME: Three hours
START: Subiaco Square
END: Subiaco Arts Centre
POINTS TO NOTE: Visit on Saturday morning to experience the lively Subi Farmers Market, Subiaco's last surviving marketplace.

Situated northwest of sprawling Kings Park, Subiaco is centred on the boulevards of Rokeby Road and Hay Street, historically home to many outlets offering tasty temptations and the odd den of iniquity – all a far cry from the suburb's Benedictine beginnings.

The pace of change in Perth is relentless, and new developments in Subiaco and elsewhere have blunted this suburb's reputation, with the loss of the Subiaco Oval and Station Street Markets. A victim of its own success, with high prices putting many Swansiders off, the suburb has also faced stiff competition in the coolness stakes from near neighbours such as Leederville,

Highgate, North Perth and reinvigorated Northbridge (see page 46).

Still, it remains a top spot for an urban stroll, during which you'll find exceptional food in some of Western Australia's very best eateries, many of them newly opened. And, in defiance of a rumoured decline, an estimated 44,000 people attended the revamped 2018 Subiaco Street Party – a free event that takes place on Rokeby Road every April – signalling, perhaps, a Subiaco renaissance.

HIP TO BE SQUARE

Subiaco's first railway station opened in 1881, a stop on the exciting Fremantle–Perth line. Skip forward a century and the tracks that once symbolised progress were a scar cleaving Perth in two. The Subi Centro project in the 1990s sent the line underground and prompted a renovation of the whole suburb.

Starting from modern-day Subiaco station, explore **Subiaco Square** ❶, a contemporary plaza that constitutes

A vibrant jacaranda tree in the suburb of Subiaco

the community hub of Subi Centro, and home to numerous places to grab brekkie and a brew, including the funky **Lion and Jaguar** (see ❶).

From here, hang a right on Brigid Road and then take a left along Dublin Close to reach **Market Square** ❷. This public park has oak trees, a gazebo, barbecues and, since 2017, the *An Gorta Mor* (Great Hunger) sculpture – a memorial to the mid-19th-century Irish Famine, a period that saw some 4,000 young orphan girls transported from Ireland to Australia's recently established colonies on 'Famine Bride Ships'.

NEW SUBIACO

The suburb's name is borrowed from an Italian town near Rome, home of a holy order of Benedictine missionaries, two of whom – Dom Serra and Dom Salvado – set up camp here in 1851, after establishing the monastic town of New Norcia (see page 102). They planted olive trees and built a church near **Lake Monger**, now a popular place for picnics, barbecues and running, which is about 500 metres/yds north of Market Square via Bunton Drive.

Exiting Market Square by Bunton Drive, walk east along Robert's Road to the **Subiaco Oval** ❸ – still standing, but redundant since the local cricket and Aussie Rules footy teams (West Coast Eagles and Fremantle) relocated to Perth Stadium (see page 54), and due to be demolished. The famous stadium gates and playing field will be saved, with the public sharing the egg-shaped space with a new school being built on Kitchener Park.

On the next block is **Mueller Park**, a leafy space named after the pioneering German botanist Ferdinand von Mueller, who did much of his best work in Australia. Head right, along Coghan Road, and then turn right again into Hay Street. Poke your open mind into the independent avant-garde **Corner Gallery** (corner of Olive and Hay streets; www.

littlewingcollective.com), which hosts exhibitions, talks, performances and installations.

ROKEBY ROAD

Continue west along Hay Street to the junction with Rokeby Road and the **Subiaco Hotel ❹** (www.subiacohotel. com.au). Built in 1897, in the midst of the gold rush, this legendary drink-

Subi Farmer's Market

ing hole is now one of Perth's most iconic pubs.

Diagonally opposite is the National Trust-listed Art Deco **Regal Theatre ❺** (www.regaltheatre.com.au), which opened as a 'hard-top' cinema in 1938, and bucked trends by morphing into a live-performance venue in 1977. Inside, the original chrome-and-jarrah fittings remain, as does the 'Crying Room' (during films, prams were once left in bays in the foyer, and if a baby started crying the parking bay number was flashed on the screen and the alerted mother could retreat to this soundproof room).

Walk south along Rokeby Road, pausing at Forrest Walk corner to look at artist Ayad Alqaragholli's *Gods Chair* sculpture. Grab a boutique brew in **Psychomug** (see ❷), or something more substantial in **Bistro Felix** (see ❸) or any of the many restaurants, pizzerias and bars lining this popular parade.

THEATRE GARDENS

Pause at the junction with Bagot Road to explore **Subi Farmer's Market** (271 Bagot Road, www.subifarmersmarket. com.au; Sat 8am–noon), which survived the onslaught of development that robbed this suburb of the sensational Asian-influenced sights and smells that once percolated around Station Street and Subiaco Pavilion Markets – both now replaced by retail

Subiaco Museum houses over 12,000 items

units housing characterless supermarkets.

Further south on Rokeby Road, in Rankin Gardens, the **Subiaco Museum** (239 Rokeby Road, tel: 08-9237 9227; Tue–Fri 1–4pm, Sat 10am–2pm) houses over 12,000 items. From here, head west along Hamersley Road to the **Subiaco Arts Centre 6** (180 Hamersley Road; tel: 08-6212 9292; www.ptt.wa.gov.au), which stages theatre productions ranging from plays and comedy to opera. Continue west to reach Daglish Railway Station, or go east to reach Kings Park (see page 31).

Subiaco Arts Centre

Food and drink

❶ LION & JAGUAR

Shop 7, Subiaco Square; tel: 08-9381 6860; daily 6.30am–3pm, also Thu–Sat from 6pm; $$

A cool café and quality caffeine imbibing spot situated in Subiaco Square, excellent for breakfast, brunch or lunch paired with a brew, juice or smoothie. It's licensed too.

❷ PSYCHOMUG

115 Rokeby Road; tel: 08-9381 7393; daily 7am–4pm, $$

A place that takes its coffee very seriously (try the tasting platter) and brings an impressive level of experimentation and innovation to both brewing and presentation (charcoal killer latte served in a skull-shaped glass anyone? Or perhaps an almond latte in an ice-cream cone?). Some food is available too, but really this is all about the coffee.

❸ BISTRO FELIX

118–120 Rokeby Road; tel: 08-9388 3077; www.bistrofelix.com.au; Mon–Sat 11.30am–late; $$$

Wine bar and restaurant offering modern European cuisine (from an à la carte to an express menu) and a large range of wines. With an in-house nutritionist there's an emphasis on healthy ingredients. In summer they feature a seafood menu.

Claisebrook Cove skyline

EAST PERTH

Once the ugly duckling to the prettier parts of the Swan, in the last decade the former industrial wasteland of East Perth has grown up and become a vibrant, cosmopolitan hub, resplendent with world-class sporting facilities and modern entertainment venues.

DISTANCE: 5.5km (3.5 miles)
TIME: A half day
START: Claisebrook
END: Perth Stadium Station
POINTS TO NOTE: This area is home to the city's biggest sports arenas, most notably the Perth Stadium, and when big games are on it will be very busy, as will surrounding cafés, bars and public transport. This route can also be cycled.

East Perth has long pulled in sports fans – being home to the WACA cricket ground, Gloucester Park, Belmont Park and the State Tennis Centre – but the area now has a jewel in its stadia tiara: the impressive shape of the Perth (Optus) Stadium. It's not all about arenas, though. The East End has come alive with numerous residential, retail and recreation-focussed projects taking shape along both banks of the river, connected by a stunning bridge that now spans the Swan.

Such developments have reinvigorated investment in East Perth, with

Claisebrook Cove a particularly popular spot. It's a far cry from the scene that would have greeted Captain Stirling when he stopped and discovered a freshwater stream here during his 1827 exploration of the Swan. He called it Clause Creek, after the ship's surgeon, but as the city expanded the area became Perth's 'East Ward', and Clause Creek morphed into Claisebrook.

CLAISEBROOK COVE

Approaching the area from Claisebrook Station, along Kensington Street and East Parade, the first thing you're going to encounter is an enigma: the *Impossible Triangle* sculpture by Brian McKay and Ahmad Abas, situated on a roundabout at the junction with Brook Street. This 13.5-metre (44ft) landmark is based on a puzzle devised by mathematician Sir Roger Penrose in the 1950s, and there are only two positions from which the triangle appears complete.

Continue south along Plain Street and duck down the steps into **Victoria**

Victoria Gardens

Gardens ❶. Situated in the pretty surrounds of Claisebrook Cove, this popular spot features free barbecues, picnic tables under the trees, a pavilion and grassy slopes leading down to the river and inlet. There are also eateries and places to grab coffee and cakes, such as the **Kinky Lizard Espresso Bar** (see ❶).

Like a lot of Perth, Claisebrook is an ancient area with powerful indigenous links. This riverbank area is known as Nganga Batta's Mooditcher (Sunshine's Living Strength) and is a place of hope and friendship. The standing stones on the foreshore form a winding trail – the **Illa Kurri Sacred Dreaming Path** – a physical narrative that describes the chain of lakes and wetlands that spanned the land prior to Perth being built; each of the granite stones is named after a lake.

Also on the foreshore is the *Charnock Woman* ceramic pavement mosaic, which tells the story of an evil woman who stole children in the Dreamtime, and the *Yoondoorup Boorn*, an old river gum that was removed, treated and returned to the site at the request of the Noongar people. Their ancestors, who camped here, used its burnt and split trunk as a hiding place for messages and goods.

These icons are part of the **East Perth Public Art Walk**, which hugs Claisebrook Cove and features 27 diverse works by as many artists, ranging from Greg James' bronze thongs (flip flops) to a 14-metre/yd-long wall mural by Joanna Lefroy Capelle depicting an allegorical account of East Perth's history from its origins in the Bibbulmun nation, via a humorous spoof on Nelson's Column (*Diver and Guard Dogs* by Russell Sheridan).

PARKS AND GARDENS

Leave the gardens by the exit that takes you out onto Royal Street, then follow Trafalgar Road south into Waterloo Crescent. On your right is East Perth Cemetery, better known as the **Pioneer Cemetery** ❷, which was opened in the colony's embryonic days and

WACA sports stadium

contains the remains of around 10,000 people of all faiths, buried before it was closed in 1899.

On your left is **Gloucester Park**  (www.gloucesterpark.com.au) where harness racing (which Australians call 'the trots') takes place. Turn left along Hale Street to reach the cricket world's famous **WACA** ❹ (www.waca. com.au; tours Mon–Fri 10am & 1pm), named after the Western Australian Cricket Association, which looks destined to host smaller games and training facilities now that big cricket and AFL matches are being staged in the Perth Stadium. The **WACA Museum** (on-site; Mon–Fri 10am–3pm; donation) features exhibits about the ground's history.

On the right is **Queen's Gardens** ❺, Perth's first public park, created in

Optus Stadium in Burswood

1899 out of clay-pits that for 50 years supplied bricks for buildings such as Perth Town Hall. Lily ponds and English trees show the garden's British influences, as does the 1927 replica of Sir George Frampton's statue of Peter Pan.

NEW VIEWS

Turn left on Hay Street and continue until you're almost beneath the Causeway leading to Heirisson Island. Here the multi-stage **Waterbank** ❻ project is gradually taking shape, which will bring more retail and residential space to the shores of the Swan.

Follow the riverside path north, passing the opposite side of Gloucester Park, until you reach the foot of the amazing $91.5 million, 65-metre (213ft)-high **Matagarup Bridge**, which connects the rest of East Perth to Burswood, a suburb bounded by the Swan River on three sides. Cross the bridge, which opened to pedestrians and cyclists in July 2018. It is festooned with over 900 metres/ yds of LED lighting, making it a spectacular sight day and night.

GAME CHANGER

Recent developments have transformed Burswood into a hub of recreation and entertainment, most obviously with the construction of the **Perth Stadium** ❼ (www.optusstadium.com.au; tours daily, outside of events, 10am, 11am, 1pm, 3pm), name-sponsored

Verdant Queen's Gardens   *The Camfield*

by Optus at the time of writing, which opened its doors in January 2018.

The stadium can seat over 60,000 people, making it Australia's third biggest sporting arena (after the Melbourne Cricket Ground and Stadium Australia in Sydney). It stages games of Aussie rules football and cricket, mostly, plus some soccer and rugby matches. Both local AFL (Australian Football League) teams, Fremantle and the West Coast Eagles, play home games here, as do the Perth Scorchers, the city's 20/20 cricket team.

BURSWOOD

Right by the stadium, **The Camfield** (see ②) is a good spot to stop for restorative beers and bites before exploring **Burswood Park** ❽ (www.burswoodpark.wa.gov.au). This was once a rubbish tip and then a golf course, but it's now a grassy expanse with wildflower displays and a heritage trail lined by statues, including one of Henry Camfield, the pioneer who settled Burswood and named it after his family home in Kent, England.

Various showy restaurants, pubs and clubs can be found south of here, but the very glitziest are clustered in the **Crown Perth** ❾ (www.crownperth.com.au) complex, where hotels, eateries and night haunts hover around a casino that never sleeps.

On the east side of the park is the **State Tennis Centre** ❿ (www.statetenniscentre.com.au), where you can hire a hardcourt for a hit around. Finish up at the **Perth Stadium Station**, or continue to **Belmont Park Racecourse**, which is just north of here, on the other side of the Graham Farmer Freeway.

Food and drink

❶ KINKY LIZARD ESPRESSO BAR

78a 20 Royal Street; tel: 08-9221 9133; www.kinkylizard.com.au; daily 6am–3pm; $$

An award-winning coffee and/or a super-food smoothie (Green Monster/Beet me Up) is the perfect way to revive your legs and open your mind before exploring the art trail that curls around Claisebrook Cove. Breakfast and lunch options are good.

❷ THE CAMFIELD

Burswood Park; tel: 08-6314 1360; www.thecamfieldbar.com.au; daily 11am–late; $$

Australia's largest pub needs all of its five bars and 175 taps when there's a big game at the massive Perth (Optus) Stadium next door. But during the week, and on non-game weekend days, this bar and restaurant, with an on-site microbrewery, is a great spot to enjoy a pint and a pizza (other pub grub available), while gazing out across the 180-degree view of the Swan River.

FREMANTLE

A short hop from Perth, on the mouth of the Swan, the port of Fremantle is a lively, independent, confident and creative city, with a proud maritime heritage, period architecture and an exciting future, epitomized by FOMO in Kings Square.

DISTANCE: 4km (2.5 miles)
TIME: A half day
START: Victoria Quay
END: Fremantle Railway Station
POINTS TO NOTE: Fremantle is a 30-minute train ride from Perth Central. Transperth buses to Fremantle leave from St George's Terrace, but go by boat if you can. The ferry from Barrack Street Jetty takes about an hour, and cruises down the Swan past some of WA's most desirable waterfront suburbs – Dalkeith, Peppermint Grove, Mosman Park and Blackwall Reach. Weekend wanderers will get to enjoy the fantastic Fremantle Markets.

FIRST PORT OF CALL

The vibrant port of Fremantle, or Freo as it's colloquially known, is often called Western Australia's second capital city. Freophiles claim it's the first. And historically – from a European perspective – they're right, because British settlement began at Fremantle several months before Perth was founded.

It was named after Captain Charles Fremantle, who planted the union flag on Arthur Head in May 1829, claiming the territory for the British Crown. This, and his resourcefulness in saving the passengers of the *Parmelia* after Captain Stirling ingloriously grounded the ship on a harbour-mouth sandbank, earned him the honour.

This is a hard-working, dock-dominated port, situated at (and shaped by) the meeting point of the Swan River and the immense Indian Ocean, yet the city has a friendly, community feel, with an almost Mediterranean flavour, and a vibrant artistic side. A wealth of 19th-century architecture can be found around its streets, but Freo is far from a living museum, as the project currently transforming Kings Square testifies.

THE QUAYSIDE

Ferries and trains deposit visitors at **Victoria Quay** (www.victoriaquay.com. au), near the berth also used by ocean

The Maritime Museum is home to numerous iconic vessels

liners and vessels making scientific expeditions to the Antarctic. The quay is a departure point for the ferry to Rottnest Island too, and it hosts various events, including child-friendly activities and regular summer screenings of **Maritime Movies** (anything with a sea theme, donation) in B-Shed.

Also on the quay are the **E-Shed Markets** (www.eshedmarkets.net.au; Fri–Sun 9am–5.30pm), where you'll find over 100 speciality shops, an international food court (open till 8pm), yoga studios, a dive academy and regular live entertainment.

SETTING SAIL

Make your way along the quay towards the sail-training ship Leeuwin (tel:

08-9430 4105; www.sailleeuwin.com). When in port, this 55-metre (180ft) three-masted barquentine is open to visitors, who can also book a half-day sailing experience. A statue of **C.Y. O'Connor** is off to the left, the visionary Irish engineer who twice achieved near-impossible feats, by creating Fremantle Harbour and building a pipeline to supply water to the goldfields of Kalgoorlie.

Continue on to the **Maritime Museum ❶** (Slip Street; tel: 08-9431 8334; www.museum.wa.gov.au/maritime; daily 9.30am–5pm). This excellent museum is an imaginatively executed exploration of Fremantle's multifaceted relationship with the ocean, and is home to the winning America's Cup yacht, *Australia II*, an Oberon class

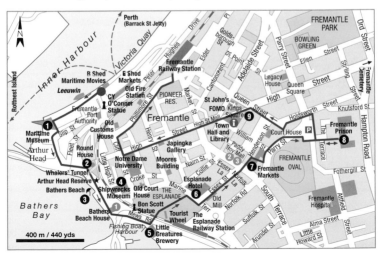

submarine – HMAS *Ovens*, the *Parry Endeavour* (a yacht that Jon Sanders took on a triple-circumnavigation of the planet), and many other iconic vessels from WA's salty history.

JAILS, WHALES AND SALTY TALES

Further around Arthur Head is the **Round House** ❷ (tel: 08-9336 6897; www.fremantleroundhouse.com.au; daily 10.30am–3.30pm; donation), Western Australia's oldest public building and its first jail, built in 1830 on the spot where Captain Fremantle claimed Western Australia for the Crown. WA's criminal element soon outgrew the capacity of the Round House and its eight small cells. A series of bigger prisons replaced it, but the Round House was used as a police lock-up until 1900,

Midnight Oil at the Fremantle Arts Centre

when it became the living quarters for the chief constable, his wife and their 10 children.

Below the jail is **Whalers' Tunnel**, which was cut through the rock in 1837 to connect the jetty with the settlement, and is now the only remnant of the whaling industry that was so crucial to the young colony. Hunters of the Fremantle Whaling Company would drag their catch through the tunnel. It was also used as an air-raid shelter in World War II. After spending long periods shut because of safety concerns, the tunnel is currently open to the public, providing an interesting access route to **Bathers Beach** ❸ – a sensational spot for a dip and a drink or bite at the **Beach House** (see ❶).

On the other side of the tracks that run behind the Beach House is the original WA Maritime Museum, now known as the **Shipwrecks Museum** ❹ (Cliff Street; www.museum.wa.gov.au; daily 9.30am–5pm, guided tours Wed & Sun 10.30am; donation) devoted to marine archaeology. Original timber and treasures from the *Batavia*, an infamous Dutch shipwreck (see page 95), are on display alongside relics from other ancient wrecks.

THE ESPLANADE

Proceed along Mews Road, passing the monument to Bon Scott (lead singer of the rock band AC/DC), who grew up here and whose final resting place in Fremantle Cemetery – heritage listed

Pastel colours at Bathers Beach House

by the National Trust – is said to be the most-visited grave in Australia and another unusual statue of a dog. On the right, a host of restaurants, ice-cream parlours and cafés line the Fishing Boat Harbour, a working dock for a 500-strong fleet.

The harbour area is a lively entertainment hub night and day. A big attraction here is **Little Creatures Brewery ⑤** (40 Mews Road; tel 08-6215 1000; www.littlecreatures.com.au; Mon–Fri 10am–late, Sat–Sun from 9am), a bar and restaurant as well as a brewery, which was set up here in a former crocodile farm in 1999 to produce a widely popular pale ale.

CAPPUCCINO STRIP

Across the Esplanade lawns, beyond the 40-metre (130ft) Tourist Wheel (www.touristwheelfremantle.com; daily 10am–9pm, until 10pm Fri and Sat), is the prominent **Esplanade Hotel ⑥** (46–54 Marine Terrace; tel: 08-9432 4811; www.hotelesplanadefremantle. com). There are five bars and restaurants behind the famous facade of this watering hole, built in the heady gold-rush days of the 1890s.

Heading away from the waterfront, Essex Street leads to **South Terrace**. Between Bannister and Parry streets this popular parade is known as 'Cappuccino Strip' because of its Italian ambiance and cornucopia of quality coffee outlets, all with tables spilling onto

Art heritage

Artists thrive in Fremantle. The city hosts an annual temporary art program to encourage artists to interact with public spaces (with amazing results), and generations of writers, actors, painters, musicians and craft people have found inspiration (and low-cost studios) in the old port buildings.

The city's own art collection (www. fremantle.wa.gov.au) boasts over 1,400 works, paintings, prints, drawings, ceramics, photographs and sculpture, mostly by Australian artists.

A bequest by businessman and art patron Claude Hotchin started the city collection in 1958. He donated 41 valuable paintings by Hans Heysen, Margaret Preston, Arthur Streeton, Rupert Bunny and others. Twenty years later the family of Kathleen O'Connor (daughter of C.Y. O'Connor) donated 43 of her works.

Many interesting pieces can be found at the **Fremantle Arts Centre** (1 Finnerty Street; tel: 08-9432 9555; www.fac.org. au; daily 10am–5pm), which includes FOUND, WA's largest curated collection of locally made artisanal wares (including prints, ceramics, woodwork, jewellery, books and textiles). Exhibitions can also be seen at civic centres like the City of Fremantle Library, Town Hall, Moore's Building and Fremantle Justice Building.

Indigenous art can be seen at **Japingka Aboriginal Art**, (47 High Street; tel: 08-9335 8265; www.japingkaaboriginalart.com).

Fremantle Markets

the street, which feels like a pedestrian mall with its low kerbs. Try the **Fremantle Bakehouse** (see ❷), or, if a cold brew is calling, you'll find some of WA's best beers in the **Sail and Anchor** (see ❸) boutique pub brewery.

MARKETS AND MARKS

Opposite the pub are the famous **Fremantle Markets** ❼ (www.fremantlemarkets.com.au; Fri 9am–8pm, Sat–Sun 9am–6pm), dating from 1897. Every weekend, over 150 unique stalls spring to life here, selling everything from fantastic food to funky threads, and buskers bash out tunes and perform tricks.

Exit from Farmer's Lane at the northern end of the markets, walk left along Parry Street, with the **Fremantle Oval**

John Gerovich statue at the Fremantle Oval

on your right. This sporting arena, which occasionally hosts concerts, is primarily used for state league Australian rules football – although they now play home games in Perth Stadium (see page 54), the AFL team the Fremantle Dockers do host some pre-season games here. It was originally used by the Pensioner Guards, who staffed the nearby prison.

FREMANTLE PRISON

From Parry Street, turn right along a pedestrianised section of Fairbairn Street which points directly at the formidable gates of **Fremantle Prison** ❽ (1 The Terrace; tel: 08-9336 9200; www.fremantleprison.com.au; daily 9am–5pm).

Australia's only World Heritage-listed building, built by convicts in the 1850s, was decommissioned as a maximum-security prison in 1991 and is now one of the WA's top tourist attractions. Myriad themed tours are available, including one of the tunnels (burrowed out by prisoners sentenced to hard labour, some of them flooded and negotiable only by boat) and another ghastly ghoulish option, which is conducted by torchlight.

BACK TO THE FUTURE

Bust out of the prison, follow the footpath alongside Parry Street car park to Holdsworth Street, turn left and head towards the centre of the city, famous for being a brilliantly preserved example of a 19th-century port streetscape. At

Fremantle Prison was built by convicts

its heart, however, a very modern beast has just been born.

Sandwiched between William and Queen streets, is **Kings Square** ❾, scene of a titanic transformation. Between 2017 and 2020, the square is undergoing a $270million facelift, changing it into an ultra-contemporary public space, resplendent with concept-heavy retail outlets, restaurants, recreational facilities and creative spaces. The planned result is **FOMO** (an acronym for 'Fremantle On My Own', with a secondary meaning 'Fear Of Missing Out').

No fear of missing anything from here, though, as it's easy to explore the older, character-soaked streets featuring Freo's finest architecture, which splinter off from the High Street on the way back towards the Round House. These include Cliff Street, Henry Street (where many of the buildings are now occupied by Notre Dame University), and Phillimore (look out for the Old Fire Station at No. 18, the Chamber of Commerce at No. 16, and the Old Customs House on the corner of Cliff Street).

A short walk up Phillimore Street leads to the magnificent station built when the Perth–Fremantle railway opened in 1881. Fast trains back to Perth leave from here.

Food and drink

❶ BATHERS BEACH HOUSE
47 Mews Road; tel: 08-9335 2911; www.bathersbeachhouse.com.au; daily 11am–late; $$
A bona fide beachfront restaurant and bar, literally three paces from the white sands of Bathers Beach, serving a full range of refreshing libations and sensational seafood in an al fresco setting.

❷ FREMANTLE BAKEHOUSE
52 South Terrace; tel: 08-9430 9592; www.fremantlebakehouse.com.au; daily 7am–6pm; $$
Family run bakery and café, offering sensational bread and breakfast (or lunch), with superb coffees and cakes too.

Kerbside dining on Freo's Cappuccino Strip at its friendly best. Their luscious lemon meringue is the perfect early afternoon pick-me-up, or try the orange and almond muffins.

❸ SAIL AND ANCHOR
64 South Terrace; tel: 08-9431 1666; www.sailandanchor.com.au; Mon–Tue 11am–11pm, Wed–Sun 10am–midnight, Sat until 1am, food until 9pm; $$$
A cathedral devoted to the worship of beer, in a heritage-listed building housing four bars with 40 cold taps and three English-style hand pumps. This pub was once the epicentre of the Matilda Bay Brewing Company (makers of such elixirs as Fat Yak, Redback and Beez Neez), and still prides itself as a craft beer institution.

PERTH'S SUBURBAN BEACHES

*Stretching a long lithe leg from Fremantle to Hillary's Boat Harbour,
via Cottesloe and Scarborough, suburban Perth's surf-combed and
sand-fringed Sunset Coast is a sensational aquatic playground – a
chain of immaculate beaches swept by Indian Ocean breakers.*

DISTANCE: 35km (22 miles)
TIME: A full day
START: South Beach, Fremantle
END: Hillary's Boat Harbour/Mullaloo
POINTS TO NOTE: You can visit South
Beach by CAT bus, and Cottesloe by
train, but the best way to explore the
whole Sunset Coast is to hire a car.
Directions are easy: keep the ocean
on your left. It's possible to drive from
Fremantle to Mullaloo in under an hour.
But don't. Stop to swim, and sit, and sip
and see. For calm conditions, choose
a day when there's an easterly breeze.
Many beaches are exposed, with little
shade or shelter – dress accordingly.
Unless you really know what you're
doing, stick to swimming on patrolled
beaches and stay between the flags.

Perth might not be on the coast, but
20-minutes' drive from the CBD lies
the spectacular Sunset Coast, where
20 idyllic Indian-Ocean beaches link
sandy hands for 50km (30 miles) north
of the Swan.

On sun-spattered weekend mornings
the entire city seems to tip towards the
ocean. Trendy Cottesloe, surfy Scarborough and family friendly Hillary's can
get hectic, but you can always find a
secluded spot somewhere along Sunset. Busier beaches have amenities
(toilets, changing rooms, picnic and
barbecue areas), and sand-side restaurants, cafés and bars – many serving
well into the evening.

FROM FREO

The Sunset Coast officially kicks off
at Cottesloe, but we start at **South
Beach ❶** – oft overlooked because of
its proximity to Fremantle (handily close,
actually, to Cappuccino Strip). An outlying reef here means no surf, but there
are views of Fremantle Marina and a
grassy area punctuated with Norfolk
pines. Several barbecue stations and
an adventure playground make this
popular with local families.

Port Beach ❷ is long and sandy,
but its backdrop is Fremantle's docks.
Strong winds discourage sunbathing,

A beautiful summer day at Leighton Beach

and signs warn swimmers of strong currents and submerged rocks. Neighbouring **Leighton Beach ❸**, home of Fremantle Surf Life Saving Club, is popular with wind- and kitesurfers. There's a small car park and a kiosk here.

Mosman Beach ❹ marks the start of **Cottesloe Reef Fish Habitat Protection Area**, which shields rare species by imposing restrictions (on jet skis and spearfishing for example) and extends to North Street. There are no facilities beyond benches, and beach access is tricky for people with disabilities or young children.

COTTESLOE

South Cottesloe Beach ❺ has a playground on a grassed area set back from the beach, but otherwise lacks amenities, which means it's often quiet (but close to Cottesloe's facilities).

Cosmopolitan **Cottesloe ❻** is this

Sunset on Swanbourne Beach

coast's main hub, popular with visitors and locals alike. Trains run between Cottesloe and the city, parking is plentiful and free (for 3 hours) – if Marine Parade is full try nearby Napier Street. Bars and cafés along Marine Parade enjoy great ocean views and fling their windows open on hot summer's days, floating the lively atmosphere into the street. Enjoy the view from **C Blu** (see ❶).

The town permanently displays 15 sculptures from previous **Sculpture by the Sea** exhibitions, held every March (www.sculpturebythesea.com/cottesloe). Lifeguards keep a watchful eye on the beach action from in front of the iconic Indiana restaurant building. Swimming conditions are generally good. An artificial reef on the far side of the groyne was created to reduce

Sculpture by the Sea

the number of surfers jostling for position on the main beach. It still gets busy, though.

Landscaped lawns rise up behind the beach, lined with Norfolk pines which provide much-needed shade. Lots of families come here as there are toilets, picnic benches, barbecues, a playground and plenty of room for children to run around. At night, make the most of the floodlit beach and enjoy fish and chips on the sand.

North Cottesloe Beach ❼ is far quieter, and only a minute's drive along Marine Parade, or a short walk along the beach. There are no facilities, limited roadside parking, and the beach is not patrolled.

SWANBOURNE AND CITY

Best-known for being clothing-optional, **Swanbourne Beach** ❽ is next to a military base and accessed by a no-through road, so has plenty of privacy, but swimming conditions can be rough. There are toilets and lots of parking. Following the road around the back of the army barracks takes you to the start of the West Coast Highway, leading to several beautiful beaches.

First is award-winning **City Beach** ❾. A large grassy area slopes gently down to a wide stretch of sand overlooked by the Surf Life Saving Club. Toilets, a kiosk and barbecue facilities mean you can comfortably spend entire days here. There are also

Scarborough has a popular beachfront running track

volleyball nets on the sand and a playground. Parking is plentiful. Duck into the **Hamptons City Beach** (see ❷) for a cold craft beer.

Expansive and attractive **Floreat Beach** ❿, in the affluent suburb of the same name, is popular with locals. It's patrolled part-time (look for red-and-yellow flags). There's a good range of amenities, including toilets, parking, free public volleyball courts, café, kiosk and large playground set under brightly coloured shades on a grassed picnic area.

Brighton Beach ⓫ is another good-sized stretch of sand, framed by attractively landscaped picnic and playground areas. Access is a short walk from the large car park through the dunes. Lifeguards patrol, surfers have their own designated area and there's a kiosk. It's a good option for those wishing to be near the attractions and amenities of Scarborough without the crowds.

SCARBOROUGH

Perhaps the premier coastal beach destination in suburban Perth, **Scarborough** ⓬ is undoubtedly the largest and most developed. Offering a wide range of waterfront accommodation, it's popular with visitors who prefer to be outside the city centre and with local surfers. The beach is patrolled, and regular surf life-saving competitions and displays are held.

Various water sports are possible, or you can kick back and watch the action from the grassed picnic area behind the dunes. The beachfront jogging track is well used, and the **Scarborough to Trigg Heritage Walk** (three short loop options, which can be combined to make a 7km/4.5-mile trek) is worth exploring. There's a good choice of bars, cafés and restaurants, and a supermarket, all a short walk from the beach. On Sunday afternoons, the bars get pretty rowdy as the legendary 'Sunday session' kicks off.

TRIGG AND MARMION MARINE PARK

South Trigg Beach has toilets and a grassed picnic area, but not much else, so most people carry on to **Trigg Beach** ⓭, another popular spot with surfers. The beach is patrolled, but strong rips can make swimming dangerous. Pop into **The Wild Fig** (see ❸) for a feed, or BYO picnic or barbecue basics and hit Clarko Reserve, a big grassy area back from the beach with a playground.

From Trigg to Burns Rock (north of Mullaloo) lies the **Marmion Marine Park** ⓮, established in 1987 to protect the reefs, lagoons and small offshore islands that run for some 5km (3 miles) along this coast. A haven for fish, dolphins, sea lions and birdlife, the park – the first of its kind in WA – offers great diving and snorkelling.

Hamptons City Beach

Dive boats depart from Hillary's Boat Harbour, but you can snorkel from the beaches, which are dramatically different from others along this stretch of coast. Gone are the dunes of Scarborough and Brighton and the wide expanses of sand at Floreat and Cottesloe; instead you'll find rocky outcrops jutting out of relatively narrow sections of sand.

Watermans Beach ⑮ boasts a good stretch of sand and interesting rock pools to explore. The water is calm in the shallows, making it good for children and inexperienced swimmers, and there's a beachside playground under shade-giving Norfolk pines. **Marmion Beach** has a small car park, but little sand.

With plenty of accommodation – and Hillary's Boat Harbour's shops, cafés and attractions right next door – **Sorrento Beach** ⑯ is a good place to come for the day. Sorrento itself has a beachside kiosk and toilets, and is patrolled by lifesavers, as winds sometimes make conditions rough.

HILLARY'S

The small, purpose-made beach at **Hillary's Boat Harbour** ⑰ is always busy with families. Boats are prohibited in parts of the marina, allowing safe swimming in calm water. There's an adventure playground on the sand, while further back from the beach is a small funfair, waterslides, minigolf and trampolines. The beach is patrolled and the surrounding precinct is filled with boutiques, souvenir shops, bars and restaurants, most of which line the timber boardwalk known as Sorrento Quay.

Behind is the excellent **Aquarium of Western Australia** (AQWA; www.aqwa.com.au; daily 10am–5pm), which recreates WA's five distinct coastal environments. The highlight is the walk-through aquarium representing the 'Shipwreck Coast', where sharks,

---

Fremantle Doctor & Sunday Sessions

Even in the sweaty grasp of high summer, when WA's temperatures regularly head somewhere north of 31°C (87°F), Perth's suburban beaches receive some blessed relief from a phenomenon known as the 'Fremantle Doctor'. This is the affectionate term given to the famous sea breeze that floats across Freo and the beaches of the Sunset Coast from the southwest each afternoon, cooling the foreshore down beautifully. It's caused by the difference in temperature between the water and the air, so the warmer the weather, the more reliable the Doctor's appointment becomes. In the dying hours of summer weekends, celebrating the arrival of the Doctor with a few cold beers in bars overlooking the ocean during in the mid-afternoon has become a tradition known as the 'Sunday Session'.

Touch pool at the Aquarium of Western Australia

loggerhead turtles and stingrays glide effortlessly over your head. There's also a touch pool, saltwater crocodiles from the tropical north and a kaleidoscope of fish from Perth's Coast. The aquarium offers mermaid classes (master a single fin) and the opportunity to swim with sharks.

TO MULLALOO

Just north of Hillary's lies **Whitfords Nodes**, a large park with picnic spaces, scenic lookouts, a children's playground and a long beach, with plenty of parking off Whitfords Avenue. **Pinnaroo Point** is another rugged coastal beach with a small grassed area and children's playground, while **Whitfords Beach** has parking (but little else). As in many places along this coast, these beaches are linked by a beachfront dual-use cycle/pedestrian path. Mullaloo Beach, towards the northern tip of the Sunset Coast, is a large, attractive spot, with picnic and barbecue facilities scattered across landscaped lawns overlooking the beach.

Food and drink

① C BLU

140 Marine Parade, Cottesloe; tel: 08-9383 5414; www.obh.com.au; daily 7.30am–9.30pm; $$$

Mere metres from the white sands of Cottesloe Beach, offering a $10 all-day breakfast and lovely lunch and dinner options. The sound of the surf, the fresh sea air and the picture-perfect sunsets all appeal to visitors' senses and complement the food.

② HAMPTONS CITY BEACH

179 Challenger Parade; City Beach; tel: 08-9385 9588; www.hamptonscitybeach.com.au; daily 7am–10pm; $$$

This beachside bar and restaurant has a great deck overlooking the white sand and rolling water of the Indian Ocean. Enjoy sunsets with craft beer, boutique wine and cocktails, or tuck into top food from a well-considered menu that celebrates the seasons and the locality (with wonderful seafood). Try the salt and pepper squid and cleanse your palate with a raspberry sorbet bombe.

③ THE WILD FIG

190 The Esplanade, Scarborough; tel: 08-9245 2533; www.thewildfig.com.au; daily 6am–10pm; $$$

More amazing views from this classy coast-hugging restaurant, open for breakfast, lunch and dinner. Enjoy excellent coffee in the morning, or ocean-side drinks with complimentary tapas a little later, before tucking into a menu that makes the most of excellent local produce, with a little international flair (try the Spanish beef arancini).

Cycling on Rottnest Island

ROTTNEST

Circumnavigate a car-free idyllic island by bicycle, pausing to play in beautiful bays – where you can snorkel in gin-clear ocean water and explore shipwrecks straight from gilded beaches – and meet famous furry local residents: the quokkas.

DISTANCE: 28km (17 miles)

TIME: A full day

START/END: Thompson Bay

POINTS TO NOTE: Take a ferry from Perth (90 minutes, Barrack Street Jetty), Fremantle (25 minutes, Victoria Quay), North Fremantle (25 minutes, Rous Head) or Hillary's Boat Harbour (45 minutes, Victoria Quay). Reasonable bikes and snorkelling equipment are available for hire on the island. Diving can be arranged from the mainland via operators including Perth Ocean Diving (www.perthocean.com). Don't touch the quokkas. More info: www.rottnestisland.com

Rotto, as the locals affectionately call Rottnest Island, is just 19km (12 miles) from Fremantle, yet it could be in another universe. A stunning place for visitors to explore, a surprisingly dark history hides behind the beautiful beaches, with the island having been used as a prison for indigenous men until 20th century.

GETTING AROUND

The island is about 11km (7 miles) long and 4.5km (3 miles) at its widest, and is best enjoyed on two wheels. With virtually no traffic, cycling is a real pleasure, and the stunning views make the hills worth the effort. Bikes can be hired through boat companies, but the best option is to pick up a steed from **Pedal and Flipper** once you're on the island (note: helmets are compulsory), where you can also hire snorkelling gear. You could get around the entire island in under three hours if you rushed, but what would be the point of that, when surrounded by such riches?

Non-bikers can loop Rottnest on the **Island Explorer** hop-on/hop-off bus service operated by Sealink (tel: 08-9325 9352; www.sealinkrottnest.com.au; tickets from visitor centre, last bus leaves at 3pm), or hike the still-evolving **Wadjemup Walking Trail** (five sections, totalling 45km/28 miles).

THOMPSON BAY

Starting from the main jetty, you'll see a

small cluster of buildings ahead, known as the Thomson Bay settlement. The buildings here are among the oldest on the island, built by indigenous prisoners incarcerated on Rottnest during the 19th century. Among these, the former hay-shed and mill has been converted into an excellent **museum** (daily 10am–3pm).

Directly opposite the end of the jetty is the **Visitor Centre** (tel: 08-9372 9732; www.rottnestisland.com; buses pick up from the central bus stop behind here), an excellent resource for planning all aspects of your visit. Behind this is a pedestrian shopping mall with a general store, post office, newsagent and cafés. To the left of the jetty are Hotel Rottnest, the Rottnest Tea Rooms and the Dome Café.

Grab a coffee here, or for something more substantial, try **Frankie's on Rotto** (see ❶) slightly further north on Somerville Drive.

LOOP THE LOOP

Rottnest has 63 beaches, so the main problem is deciding which one to head to first. One advantage of staying for two days is the ability to do a round-island riding recce on the first day, before returning to your favourite spot the next. Even if you're here for one day only, though, a cycling circumnavigation is the best way to get a taste of the island.

Taking a clockwise route and heading south along Parker Point Road will

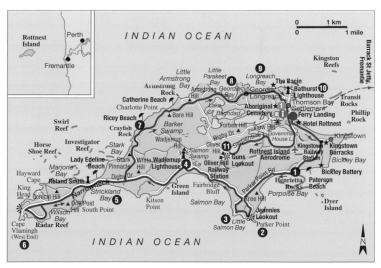

Aboriginal prisoner cemetery

Rottnest rewound

Aboriginal habitation of Rottnest dates back 30,000 years, well beyond the island's separation from the mainland 6,500 years ago. Nyungar call the island *Wadjemup* (place where spirits come to rest) and it's enormously culturally significant.

Dutchman Willem de Vlamingh put the island on European maps in 1696. Mistaking quokkas for rodents he named it 'Rottenest' (rats' nest).

Early English settlers from the Swan River Colony arrived in 1829. Skirmishes with the Nyungar became frequent and soon large numbers of indigenous men were imprisoned.

From 1838, Aboriginal prisoners from the mainland were sent to Rottnest, and in 1841 it officially became an open prison, which operated until 1904. During this time, 3,700 men and boys (8–80 years of age) were incarcerated. Hundreds died and were buried in unmarked graves.

When the prison closed Rottnest opened to the public. In 1917 the island was declared an A-Class Reserve, so land couldn't be leased or sold. Campsites were built in the 1920s, along with a general store and tearooms. By the 1930s, ferries were delivering hundreds of holidaymakers.

During World War II the military occupied Rottnest. Guns were installed at Bickley Battery and Oliver Hill, to protect Fremantle, and barracks and a railway were built. Troops withdrew in 1945, and visitors returned.

lead you past turnings to **Kingstown Barracks** and **Bickley Battery**, military remnants from when Rottnest was on high alert during World War II (see box), tasked with protecting the port of Fremantle, which was a secret submarine base. Both are worth a look. Bickley once bristled with two 6-inch guns, and the Barracks offers budget accommodation.

The first sand of note is at **Paterson Beach**. Continue around to **Henrietta Rocks ❶**, where the wreck of *The Shark* lies within easy swimming distance (50 metres/yds) of the beach. It can be viewed from the beach too, from where it looks like a drowned crane, but snorkellers can obviously get closer, and meet the myriad sea creatures that now live amid *The Shark's* skeleton (always be extremely careful around artificial structures in the water).

On the other side of Porpoise Bay, just past **Jeannies Lookout** (a stunning viewpoint) is **Parker Point ❷**, where a 2km (1.2-mile) -long **snorkelling trail** has been laid out beneath the waves, featuring plaques on the seabed with information about the abundant flora and fish life in the area. **Little Salmon Bay ❸** is another sensational swimming and snorkelling spot.

Continue around the broad arc of big **Salmon Bay**, where conditions are good for surfing. Just past Fairbridge Bluff there's a turning right, leading inland and up a hill, to **Wadjemup Lighthouse ❹** (tours available; children under five not permitted inside).

Beach fun at The Basin

There's been a lighthouse here since 1849, but when the current tower was built in 1896, it became Australia's first rotating-beam lighthouse. The view is cracking, and there's a café next door.

Return to the coast and continue west around the island, skirting **Strickland Bay** ❺, which boasts Rottnest's most reliable surf break. Cross the **Narrowneck**, where you'll see the dunes of **Lady Edeline** Beach and **Roland Smith Memorial**, dedicated to a local man who saved many ships from coming to grief on the treacherous rocks that surround the island, by installing navigation markers.

Along Digby Drive and beyond Conical Hill is the island's most westerly point: barren, exposed and evocative **Cape Vlamingh** ❻, the very extremity of which you can reach via a boardwalk, which curls around Fish Hook Bay. After doing a little lap of Aitken Way head back across the Narrowneck and begin the return route.

Beyond **Rocky Bay** and **Stark Bay** (the latter with an exposed reef break and consistent surf), just past Crayfish Rock, is **Ricey Beach** ❼, a sensational swimming and snorkelling spot.

A golden chain of beautiful, reef-ringed beaches extends along the island's north shore, including **City of York Beach** named after a three-masted sailing ship that sank here in 1899, almost in eyeshot of Fremantle, having sailed all the way from San Francisco, (its anchor is on display by Rottnest's Main Jetty) and **Catherine Beach**. Continue over Armstrong Hill to **Little Parakeet Bay** and **Geordie**

Bay ❽, where more sheltered swimming conditions can be found.

Past Point Clune is **Longreach Bay** ❾, where **The Basin** is the closest really decent beach to Thompson Bay, and consequently the place for which many day visitors make a beeline.

Near **Pinky Beach** you'll see **Bathurst Lighthouse** ❿, established in 1900 in response to the *City of York* disaster. Off to the right here is the Aboriginal cemetery, a sombre spot where the remains of an estimated 370 Nyungar men and boys are buried – some victims of disease, others who were hanged (see boxed text).

If time permits, head over **View Hill**, wend through the lakes along Digby Drive, then take a left to reach **Oliver Hill** ⓫, where you can explore the gun battery and a maze of tunnels used by the military in World War II (tours daily 10am, 11am, noon, 1pm and 2pm).

Food and drink

❶ **FRANKIE'S ON ROTTO**

342 Somerville Drive; tel: 0431 735 090; www.frankiesonrotto.com.au; 8am–8pm; $$

A top spot for coffee, breakfast, lunch or dinner with a selection of pizzas, pastas and salads made on site. Eat in, with BYO wine, or order take-away (delivery across the island, 4–7pm autumn–winter, longer in spring–summer). Try the loaded fries for a carb hit after cycling and swimming all day.

The Swan River

SWAN VALLEY

Explore upstream along the Swan River for an extraordinary epicurean experience through the vineyards and wild corners of an area just outside of Perth, which has been producing palate-pleasing bounty since before European settlement started in 1829.

DISTANCE: 60km (37 miles)
TIME: A full day
START/END: Guildford
POINTS TO NOTE: This route requires a vehicle. Directions begin and end in the gateway town of Guildford, a 25-minute drive from Perth city centre, towards the airport on Route 51 (Guildford Road) or Highway 94 (the Great Eastern). Regular trains serve Guildford from Perth Railway Station (30 minutes). You can also travel along the Swan Valley by boat, with trips leaving daily from Barrack Street. Myriad organised bus tours incorporating wine tasting can also be arranged from Perth. The route can easily be driven in a day – although there are numerous accommodation options in the valley, from boutique B&Bs to hotels and budget options. For more information about the region, see www.swanvalley.com.au.

Residents of Perth might live in one of the world's most isolated cities, but many feel they have everything they could possibly need right on their doorstep: ocean and beaches to the west and – in the verdant hills and vineyard-rich valleys leading inland to the northeast – a fantastically fecund, fruitful wild garden that puts world-class food on their tables and keeps their glasses considerably more than half full.

From the gardens of Guildford to the art-strewn and history soaked bushland of Yagan Memorial Park, the upper reaches of the Swan Valley are characterised by lush vineyards and towns redolent of a bygone age. A little further afield are the Perth Hills, where you'll find John Forrest National Park, waterfalls and botanical gardens.

GUILDFORD

Start in one of WA's earliest settlements. **Guildford ❶** was established in 1829, the same year the Swan River Colony was founded, upstream from Perth in the Swan Valley. Half-an-hour from the city by train or road, it's the

most accessible and appealing of the surrounding districts; if you only do one out-of-town trip, make this it. A further five minutes by car will take you through the vineyards of WA's oldest wine area, where wineries, breweries, restaurants and tourist attractions welcome visitors year round.

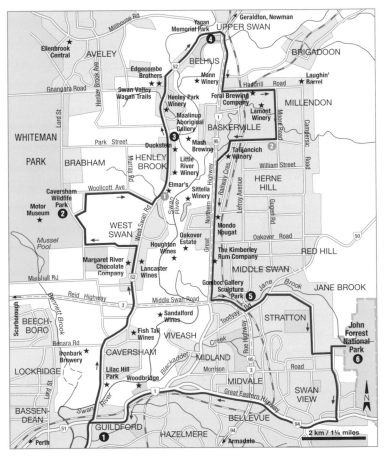

Entrance to Sandalford Wines

Guildford is easily explored on foot. Opposite the railway station, a parade of antiques shops lines James Street between the enormous Federation-style **Guildford Hotel**, recently restored after a devastating fire, and the Art Deco **Town Hall**. Most of the period homes and public buildings are around Stirling Square, off Meadow Street, between the railway and river.

On Meadow Street you'll find the town jail, gallows and courthouse, housing the award-winning **Swan Valley Visitor Centre** (Old Guildford Courthouse, corner of Meadow and Swan streets; tel: 08-9207 8899; www.swanvalley.com.au; daily 9am–4pm), which provides information about every aspect of the region, plus maps of short walking trails around town.

Lancaster Wines

As well as the Visitor Centre, the courthouse contains a collection of costumes and personal possessions, reflecting life in the town in the early 19th century. Nearby on Swan Street is the **Rose and Crown** (see page 114), a Federation-period hotel with a fine restaurant.

Meadow Street becomes West Swan Road when it crosses the river at Barker's Bridge, by Lilac Hill Park cricket ground (where visiting international teams play a warm-up match against a WA President's XI every year), and this is the starting point for valley adventures.

GOING WILD

Travel north along West Swan Road, passing a left-hand turn along Benara Road to **Ironbark Brewery** (55 Benara Road; tel: 08-9377 4400; www.iron-barkbrewery.com.au; daily), a microbrewery producing speciality beers, regular pilsner, iron bock and wheat, as well as fruity cherry ale and a ginger beer. There's a restaurant here, too.

Just before the Reid Highway is a turn-in to the right for **Sandalford Wines**. Cross the highway, go past **Lancaster Wines** (see box) on your right and **The Margaret River Chocolate Company** on the left before turning left on Harrow Street, which takes you to the edge of Whiteman Park, a 4,000-hectare (9,800-acre) expanse of bushland.

Chocolate factory   *Explore Swan Valley Vineyards*

Turn right and drive along Lord Street, which shadows the eastern edge of Whiteman Park, before taking a left into the trees, along Whiteman Drive East to **Caversham Wildlife Park** ❷ (tel: 08-7111 1028; www.caversham wildlife.com.au; daily 9am–5.30pm), the best place for native wildlife spotting for visitors too short of time to truly 'go bush'. As well as grey and red kangaroos, look out for the rare white kangaroo (albino versions of the red) and white Tammar wallaby.

Caversham aims to represent wildlife from all corners of Australia, much of which is unique to the continent. The names alone are fascinating: the southwest section features the walleroo, rock wallaby and quokka; the southeast has gliders, potteroos, wombats, Tasmanian devils and koalas. Whiteman Park has many other attractions too, including a pool and playpark.

GERMAN ALE AND INDIGENOUS ART

Head right on Youle-Deane Road, taking Everglades Avenue (left) and Woollcott Avenue (right) to meet the West Swan Road, then go left. Two tasty Teutonic-themed breweries and restaurants are found here: **Elmar's in the Valley** (see ❶) and **Duckstein** (9,720 West Swan Road; tel: 08-9296 0620; www.duckstein.com.au; Sun–Thu 11am–5pm, Fri–Sat 11am–late) a German microbrewery that makes beer

Hear it on the grapevine

Australian wine is soaring in popularity at home and abroad. At the cellar door of Swan Valley's vineyards, expect handmade wines of superior depth, style and quality. Every winery on the map is worth a visit; the following is just a taste.

Lancaster Wines
5228 West Swan Road; tel: 08-9250 6461; www.lancasterwines.com.au; daily
With some of the valley's oldest vines and most knowledgeable staff, Lancaster offers all the grape types that grow best in Swan Valley (shiraz, cabernet sauvignon, verdelho, chenin blanc and chardonnay). Try an Old Vines Shiraz and a late-picked chenin dessert wine.

Talijancich
26 Hyem Road; tel: 08-9296 4289; www.taliwine.com.au; phone ahead for tasting
Famous for fortified wines: tawny and vintage port, muscat and tokay. Its verdelho is superb, as is the Old Vine (1932) Shiraz. Tastings and tours on the first Saturday of the month.

Houghton Wines
Dale Road, Middle Swan; tel: 08-9274 9540; www.houghton-wines.com.au; daily
A valley stalwart, Houghton is WA's largest commercial winery. It has an extensive stable of wines and a restaurant. Its most famous winemaker was Jack Mann, whose family now run Mann Wines, who produced white Burgundy, Australia's best-selling bottled wine.

Belvoir Amphitheatre, a stunning outdoor music venue

according to the *Bavarian Purity Law* of 1516, using only pure water, malt and hops. The beer is accompanied by traditional German food, and sometimes the strains of a mechanical oompah band.

A little further on is the **Maalinup Aboriginal Gallery** ❸ (10,070 West Swan Road, Henley Brook; tel: 08-9296 0711/0411 12 450; www.maalinup.com.au; daily 10am–5pm; charge for activities) where you can meet representatives of the Wardandi people, see art and experience cultural performances in the form of dancing, didgeridoo playing, storytelling and bush-tucker tasting sessions. 'Maali' is the Wardandi word for the black swan, and 'up' means 'place of', so the indigenous people called this region the place of the swan long before colonist coined the name for the valley, and they have been enjoying its bounty for millennia.

Continue into the Upper Swan, via **Henley Park Winery** (www.henleywine.com) and **Edgecombe Brothers** (corner of West Swan and Gnangara Road; tel: 08-9296 4307; www.edgecombebrothers.com.au), where the Edgecombe family complement their long-established vines with asparagus, honey, table grapes, preserves and wine-derived speciality ice cream.

A turning on the right just past here leads across the river to Belvoir Amphitheatre (tel: 08-9296 3033; www.belvoir.net.au/amphitheatre), a stunning outdoor venue to experience live music.

You'll soon reach **Yagan Memorial Park** ❹, named after a Noongar warrior who was murdered here for a £30 reward by two teenage brothers in 1833. A bounty had been placed on Yagan's head after he was accused of killing two brothers, who allegedly raped an Aboriginal woman who may have been his sister. After being betrayed and shot in the back (an act widely condemned across the colony) his head was taken to Britain to be displayed as a curiosity. After years of campaigning by the indigenous community it was finally returned in 1997, and in 2010 was buried at a secret location in this park, which had been created and populated with several works of art to commemorate his legacy.

At the major T-junction, turn right along the Great Northern Highway to head south, back towards Guildford, quickly crossing the Swan River. **Mann Winery** is off to the right, along Memorial Avenue.

Turn left along Haddrill Road to check out Feral Brewing, and then swing right on Moore Road. On the corner of Bisdee Road is **Fig Tree Estate Winery** ❷ (www.figtreeestate.com.au) and opposite is **Lamont Winery**, owned by one of WA's most highly-regarded wine and gourmet food families, and connected with restaurants across the state.

Continue along Moore Road, turn right on Padbury Avenue, cross the railway tracks and pass **Talijancich winery** (see box) before rejoining the Great Northern Highway and going south. En

Houghton Winery

route, look out for a right-hand turn to **Houghton Wines** (see box).

Go left at the junction with the Roe Highway, then left again on Toodyay Road. Just across the railway tracks, yet another left turn leads to **Gomboc Gallery Sculpture Park ❺** (50 James Road, Middle Swan; tel: 08-9274 3996; www.gomboc-gallery.com.au; Wed–Sun 10am–5pm). Established in 1982, this ever-changing and dramatically diverse park features sculptures by emerging artists of all disciplines, with a new major exhibition staged each month. There's an indoor gallery, and the park sprawls across 4.5-hectares (11-acres).

Continue along Toodyay Road before turning right on Talbot Road and driving through suburbia until you hit a T-junction with Morrison Road. Going left here leads to the edge of **John Forrest National Park ❻** (tel: 08-9290 6100; https://parks.dpaw.wa.gov.au/park/john-forrest; daily) The park has two stunning waterfalls, Hovea and National Park Falls, countless kilometres of trails through wild jarrah forest, and is home to 10 species of native mammal, 91 species of bird, 23 species of reptile, 10 species of frog and 500 species of wildflowers.

At the northern edge of the park is the open-air Redhill Auditorium www.redhillauditorium.com.au), another superb under-the-stars venue to catch a gig. From the original entry point, the Swan View Road takes you south, where a right turn on Old York Road meets the Great Eastern Highway, which leads all the way back to Guildford.

Food and drink

❶ ELMAR'S IN THE VALLEY

8,731 West Swan Road, Henley Brook; tel: 08-9296 6354; www.elmars.com.au; Wed–Sun lunch only, Fri–Sun lunch and dinner; $$$

Elmar and wife Annette have created their own microbrewery and restaurant serving great German food, well beyond the sausage (which is still legendary). Every dish is prepared with care, from the pumpernickel bread to the schweinebraten – (German-style roast pork), schnitzels and zweibel (onion) sauce.

❷ FIG TREE ESTATE WINERY

100 Bisdee Road, Millendon; tel: 08-9296 2669; www.figtreeestate.com.au; Sat–Sun 11am–4.30pm, and by appointment; $$

A fresh face in the valley of the vines, Fig Tree is a family owned winery which began operation in 2011 – growing verdelho, shiraz and grenache grapes – and first opened its cellar door in 2014. Since then it has been beguiling guests with small-lot, traditionally made fine wines (the sparkling chenin is a crisp, citrus-soaked wonder), friendly service, wood-fired pizzas and sumptuous cheese platters, complete with figs when the 100-year-old fig tree is in fruit (Feb–Mar).

Penguin Island, Rockingham

SOUTH OF PERTH

It's possible to meet most of the wildlife of Western Australia on this one-day whirlwind escapade, from kayaking around islands populated by penguins and sea lions, and swimming with dolphins, to encountering echidnas, 'roos and cockatoos in waterfall-punctuated parks.

DISTANCE: 205km (127 miles)
TIME: A full day
START/END: Perth
POINTS TO NOTE: You will need a vehicle to do the full route. Rockingham and Mandurah are served by trains from/to Perth (32 and 49 minutes from Elizabeth Quay). While it's possible to do the circuit in one day, spending two will allow more time to explore. An entry fee (AU$13 per standard vehicle) is payable at Yalgorup and Serpentine national parks.

It speaks volumes about the quality of the beaches north of Fremantle that arcs of golden sand like Coogee, which would be celebrated in destinations less spoilt for choice, barely get a look in.

ROCKINGHAM AND SHOALWATER ISLANDS

There are several seafront attractions in **Rockingham** ❶. Cape Peron, with protected coves and good snorkelling conditions, is worth exploring, and beachside Bell and Churchill Park is a top spot to spend the day. Vista-endowed eateries like **Latitude 32** (see ❶) offer refreshments. Nearby is the **Catalpa Memorial**, which marks the daring 1876 escape of six Irish political prisoners from the penal colony.

Rockingham Beach is a protected spot, good for snorkelling with kids, while more experienced bubble blowers head to the West Coast Dive Park, which is rich in fish, coral and wrecks.

Rockingham Visitor Centre (19 Kent Street; tel: 08-9592 3464; rockinghamvisitorcentre.com.au; Mon–Fri 9am–5pm, Sat–Sun 9am–4pm) provides details about adventures ranging from sky diving to SCUBA diving.

MANDURAH

Hit the highway south to **Mandurah** ❷, which exudes a permanent holiday atmosphere, partly because so much of the city overlooks canals, the ocean or the Peel Inlet. Many of its restaurants,

Mandurah foreshore

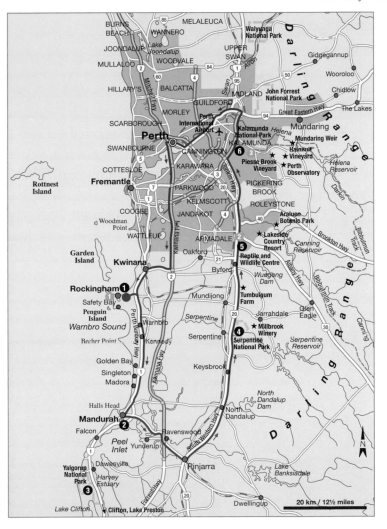

Hiking in Serpentine National Park

craft shops, art galleries and cultural buildings are set around magical Mandjar Bay.

Inexpensive estuary and canal cruises are an excellent way to explore; several operators can be found on the jetty close to Mandurah Art Centre. Skippers are skilled at finding the dolphins that live in the estuary, and simply seeing them surf and barrel-roll ahead of your cruiser is worth the fare.

Fishing is also popular, especially crabbing. On summer weekends thousands hunt for blue mannas, wading the shallows with scoop nets. The **Mandurah Crab Festival** (www.crabfest.com.au; March) is a major annual event.

YALGORUP

Mandurah's southern boundary is **Yalgorup National Park** ❸ (tel: 08-9303 7750; https://parks.dpaw.wa.gov.au/park/yalgorup; daily), which has a chain of about ten lakes (the Noongar word Yalgor means 'lake' and 'up' means 'place') and is a sanctuary for water birds and wildlife.

However, it's a colony of living, rare, rock-like creatures that makes Yalgorup's Lake Clifton special. Thrombolites date back 3.5 billion years, and like the stromatolites of Hamelin Pool (see page 97), are among Earth's earliest known lifeforms. Access is via the Coast Road, 25km (16 miles) south of Mandurah, indicated by a large brown sign for the Lake Clifton platform, an observation walkway built across the shallows.

EXPLORING INLAND

Roll around the Peel Inlet to Pinjarra. **Peel Zoo** (Sanctuary Drive; tel: 08-9531 4322; www.peelzoo.com.au; Mon–Fri 10am–4pm, Sat–Sun 9am–5pm) is on your left as you approach the town.

Head north along the South Western Highway, pausing to explore **Serpentine National Park** ❹ (tel: 08-9525 2128; https://parks.dpaw.wa.gov.au/park/serpentine; daily) a popular 4,387-hectare (10,840-acre) wild reserve, home to spectacular **Serpentine Falls**, an enigmatic place of importance to the Noongar people for millennia.

Just 55km (34 miles) from Perth, it gets busy. There are barbecues here, and a mobile food-and-drink outlet serves the car park. Numerous walking trails provide an opportunity to encounter bouncing mobs of kangaroos. Other resident animals include echidna, mardo, quenda, brushtail possum, western brush-wallaby, and over 70 species of birds. From July to November the park erupts with blooming wildflowers, with hundreds of species including spider orchids, giant sundew, greenhoods and triggerplants.

ARMADALE

Just before Armadale, the excellent **Reptile and Wildlife Centre** ❺ (308

Kalamunda

South Western Highway; tel: 08-9399 6927; www.armadalereptilecentre.com.au; daily 10am–4pm) rescues, rehabilitates and shows native reptiles and snakes, as well as bats, eagles, dingoes and other creatures.

Around Armadale there are various points of interest, including an **Aboriginal Interpretation Centre** at Champion Lakes, where you can learn about Noongar culture, heritage and history; and several parks (Araluen Botanic, Bungendore) nice for picnicking. For food in town, try **Cantina & Grill** (see ②).

KALAMUNDA

Take the Tonkin Highway towards **Kalamunda ❻**, where early European settlement of the region can be explored at the **History Village** (56 Railway Road; tel: 08-9293 1371; www.kalamun dahistoricalsociety.com; Mon–Thu & Sat 10am–3pm, Sun 1.30–4.30pm), where an antique post office, school, settler's cottage, workshops and two railway stations are all equipped with original artefacts and furnishings.

This region is rich in natural attractions and walking trails, ranging from short tracks in **Fred Jacoby Forest Park** to the 1,000km (620-mile) **Bibbulmun Track**, one of the world's great long-distance trails, which starts in Kalamunda before meandering through the wild southwest all the way to Albany (see page 86). For options, including single-day walks without a pack, contact the **Bibbulmun Track Foundation** (tel: 08-9481 0551; www.bib bulmuntrack.org.au) The equally epic **Munda Biddi cycle trail** (www.mund abiddi.org.au; see page 25) runs from Mundaring to Albany and passes through Jarrahdale.

Food and drink

① LATITUDE 32

The Boardwalk Shop 7 & 8, 1 Railway Terrace, Rockingham; tel: 08-9592 8881; www.l32.net.au; daily 11am–late; $$$
The very best from surf and turf is on the menu here at this American-influenced, but locally sourced, steak and seafood joint, right by the ocean shore. Try the seafood fettuccine. The bar has happy hour on Fridays.

② CANTINA & GRILL

Shop 9, 10 Orchard Avenue, Armadale; tel: 08-6594 1786; www.cantinaandgrill.com.au; Sun–Wed 11am–9pm, Thu–Sat until 9.30pm; $$
A versatile and comprehensive Mediterranean-influenced menu with lots of seafood options greets diners here. Portions are particularly generous, and the meat platter is great value. Try the paella a la Valencia (shellfish, chicken and Spanish sausage over saffron rice).

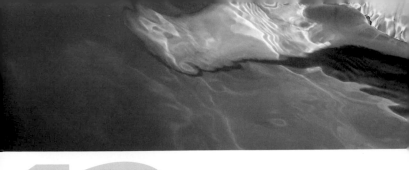

MARGARET RIVER AND SOUTHWEST

Margaret River is famous for vines and fine wines, but beyond the grapes this great escape visits the cape where the Indian and Southern oceans collide, karri forests thrive, caves honeycomb dramatic limestone landscapes, and surfers play amid migrating whales.

DISTANCE: 1,150km (715miles)
TIME: Three days
START/END: Perth
POINTS TO NOTE: This route requires use of a vehicle. Although it can be done in three days, take as much time as you can spare. Accommodation is plentiful and diverse in the southwest (see page 115). If time is tight, Regional Express Airlines (REX; www. rex.com.au) offer flights between Perth and Albany, where there are a number of car-hire companies.

WA's southwest corner is every epicure's ultimate destination, with superb vineyards, abundant olive groves, boutique breweries, craft cheesemakers and fine-food producing farms. But the region is also rich in wildlife and outdoor adventure amid an epic environment, where hiking and biking trails wend through ancient karri forests, deep caves gape from the limestone landscape and serious swell rolls into a much-storied coastline where the South Pacific meets the Indian Ocean around Cape Leeuwin.

BUNBURY

Take the Kwinana Freeway between Mandurah and Pinjarra (see page 78), segueing onto the Forrest Highway across the Murray River, to pass through Myalup State Forest and reach **Bunbury ❶**, WA's third-largest population centre. **No Oneforty** (see ❶) is a good place for brunch.

Visit the **Dolphin Discovery Centre** (Koombana Beach; tel: 08-9791 3088; www.dolphindiscovery.com.au; daily 8am–4pm) to meet a community of bottlenose dolphins that visits the beach daily to feed; you can stand within an arm's reach of the mammals. Dolphin cruises depart daily November–April, and the centre offers popular swimming-with-dolphins experiences.

For birdlife, head to the **Big Swamp Reserve** (Prince Phillip Drive), home to over 70 species of waterfowl, and crossed by boardwalks leading to hides.

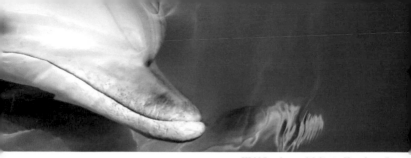

Wild Bottlenose dolphin in Koombana Bay

Information about the wetlands is available from the **Big Swamp Wildlife Park** (tel: 08-9721 8380; www.bunburywildlifepark.com.au; daily 10am–5pm) across the road. The park itself has many native animals.

GEOGRAPHE BAY

Drive 30 minutes south to **Busselton ❷**, gateway to the Margaret River Wine Region, one of the state's top destinations. The town's north-facing (therefore

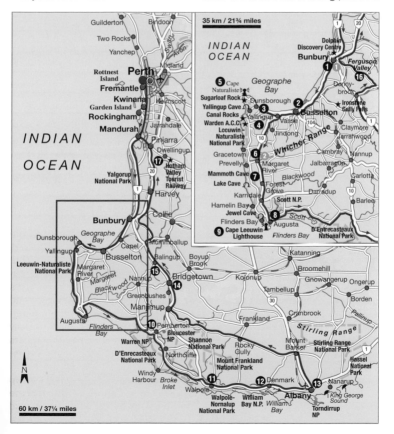

Bunker Bay on Cape Naturaliste is incredibly beautiful

protected) aspect on Geographe Bay makes it perfect for swimming.

Much-photographed mile-long **Busselton Jetty** (www.busseltonjetty.com.au; daily 24 hours) is the southern hemisphere's longest wooden pier (1,840 metres/6,037ft). The electric Jetty Train chugs all the way to the end, where an **Underwater Observatory** (tel: 08-9754 0900; daily, Sep–Apr 8am–6pm, May–Sept 9am–5pm), dunks visitors 8 metres (26ft) below sea level for amazing views of fish and coral. Tickets are available from the nearby boatshed-style **Interpretive Centre** (daily 8.30am–6pm), which tells the jetty's history and screens live underwater action from beneath the jetty via a marine cam.

CAPE NATURALISTE

Just west of Busselton, along Caves Road, are the townships of **Dunsborough ❸** and **Yallingup ❹**. Surrounded by vineyards, this booming area is popular for weekend getaways. Half- and full-day winery tours are available through operators such as **Taste the South Winery Tours** (www.tastethesouth.com.au), but all the best wineries are well-signposted from Caves Road between Yallingup and Gracetown.

Art centres also abound, including **Gunyulgup Galleries** (Gunyulgup Valley; tel: 08-9755 2177; www.gunyulgupgalleries.com.au; daily 10am–5pm). **Yallingup Galleries** (www.yallingupgalleries.com.

au) and jewellery specialist **John Miller Design** (www.johnmillerdesign.com) are both on Marrinup Drive, Yallingup.

Six kilometres (4 miles) south of Yallingup, on Injidup Springs Road, is **Wardan Aboriginal Cultural Centre** (tel: 08-9756 6566; Wed–Mon 10am–4pm), which explains the culture of the Wardani, traditional custodians of the area. In addition to a gallery, it offers a bush-based story trail, tool-making and spear-throwing workshops, and music and dance performances.

BEACHES

Dunsborough has beautiful beaches, perfect for families. For more secluded sand, follow Naturalist Road, northeast of Dunsborough, to Meelup, Eagle Bay and Bunker Bay. Smith's Beach, off Caves Road and Canal Rocks Road south of Yallingup, is the area's best surfing spot.

Naturaliste Road also leads to the tip of **Cape Naturaliste ❺**, with a lighthouse (open daily 9.30am–4pm), built in 1903. The 155km (96-mile) **Cape-to-Cape Walk** leads from here to Cape Leeuwin Lighthouse (see page 85), winding through the Leeuwin-Naturaliste National Park.

WINE

Continue south along Caves Road, turning left at Carters Road to **Margaret River ❻**, home to some of Australia's top wineries, including **Vasse**

Stalactites in Ngilgi Cave　　　　　　　　*Wild humpback whale*

Felix (www.vassefelix.com.au) and **Voyager Estate** (www.voyagerestate. com.au), both a 10-minute drive from town. Begin tours at the Margaret River Regional Wine Centre, in the centrally located **Margaret River Visitor Centre** (100 Bussell Highway; tel: 08-9780 5911; www.margaretriver.com; daily 9am–5pm). It holds regular free varietal wine-tastings and can supply maps to all the wineries in the area.

The Visitor Centre also provides information on attractions like the **Eagles Heritage Wildlife Centre** (Boodjidup Road; tel: 08-9757 2960; www.eaglesheritage.com.au; flight displays 11am and 1.30pm) and hiking trails through local karri forest. Margaret River is a big mountain-biking destination; contact Dirty Detours (www.dirtydetours.com) for guided rides. When you've earned a thirst, hit the **Brewhouse** (see ❷).

CAVES

Stretching from Busselton to Augusta, the Leeuwin-Naturaliste Ridge is honeycombed with over 150 limestone caves. Highlights include **Yallingup Ngilgi Cave** (daily 9am–5pm; guided tours and longer adventure experiences available), where Aboriginal legends abound; massive **Mammoth Cave** ❼ (21km/13 miles south of Margaret River; daily 9am–5pm; self-guided tour possible); the reflections in **Lake Cave** (Caves Road, 25km/15 miles south of Margaret River; daily 9am–5pm; guided tours only) and the spectacularly colossal chambers of **Jewel Cave** (8km/5 miles north of Augusta; daily 9am–5pm; guided tours only).

WHALES

Nestled on Flinders Bay at the mouth of the Blackwood River and the southernmost end of the Margaret River Wine Region, **Augusta** ❽ is a place to unwind by swimming, walking or taking a leisurely river cruise.

It also has superb whale watching. Southern rights and occasionally rare blue whales visit during their yearly migration up WA's coast. Whales stay from May to August, with up to 200 playing in Flinders Bay during peak season. Join a daily tour with **Naturaliste Charters** (tel: 08-9755 2276; www.whales-australia.com.au), who also run killer whale–spotting trips to Bremer Canyon, just past Albany.

Cape Leeuwin Lighthouse ❾ (Leeuwin Road, south of Augusta; tours available daily), situated near the meeting point of the Indian and Southern oceans, is a famous landmark and a wonderful place to watch whales from dry land.

TREE CLIMBING

On the far side of Flinders Bay is **Pemberton** ❿, springboard for exploring the region's national parks (https://parks. dpaw.wa.gov.au) and towering karri forests – from the treetops if you're brave enough to climb up to platforms once used to spot fires.

Visit **Gloucester National Park** (3km/2 miles east) to climb a spiral staircase around the Gloucester Tree to a 53-metre (174ft) -high lookout; **Diamond Tree** (15-minute drive north of Pemberton, on South Western Highway), where the eponymous tree has a 49-metre (160ft) -high platform; and **Warren National Park** (15-minute drive from Pemberton on Vasse Highway), where the Dave Evans Bicentennial Tree has 165 pegs leading to a 65-metre (213ft) -high vantage point. Fishing for trout and marron (freshwater crayfish) is also popular here.

THE GREAT SOUTHERN

Head southeast from Pemberton to **Walpole** ⓫, located amid Walpole-Nornalup National Park and boasting thick forests, beaches and a rugged coast.

The thrilling **Valley of the Giants Treetop Walk** (tel: 08-9840 8263; www.valleyofthegiants.com.au; daily 9am–5pm), where a 600-metre/yd-long boardwalk passes though the canopy of the surrounding tingle forest, lies 13km (8 miles) east of Walpole along the South Coast Highway. Occasional night tours are available. At ground level, the **Ancient Empire Walk** (free) follows boardwalks around the base of the wide-girth trees.

After Walpole, the South Western Highway becomes the South Coast Highway and continues east to **Denmark** ⓬, a pretty riverside town surrounded by scenic drives. These include the **Scotsdale Tourist Drive** (34km/21 miles), which passes great wineries, art galleries and local producers to end at the famous Greens Pool in the William Bay National Park.

ALBANY

Scenically situated on King George Sound, **Albany** ⓭ was once a whaling town. Hunting ceased in 1978, but a former whaling station on Cheynes Beach now houses **Whale World** (Frenchman Bay Road; www.discoverybay.com.au/historic-whaling-station; daily 9am–5pm), which explains the old industry. Southern right and humpback whales still visit between June and October, and instead of chasing these magnificent mammals with harpoons, local skippers now offer whale-watching experiences. Operators include **Albany Whale Tours** (www.albanywhaletours.com.au).

Nearby **Torndirrup National Park** (free) hugs the rugged coast, and features 'the Gap' an awe-inspiring 24-metre (79ft) chasm, which visitors can view from the safety of a steel cage on the cliff's edge. The Natural Bridge is a large granite rock that's been eroded over time to create a large arch.

Back in town, past Australia's largest wind farm, **HMAS Perth** is visible in the shallows of King George Sound, her mast rising out of the water. Scuttled in 2001, the vessel is a decent dive and snorkelling site. Some of WA's most beautiful beaches lie close to Albany, among them **Nanarup Beach** (off the Lower Kalgan Road, 25km/15 miles east of town), pop-

Denmark

ular with surfers; **Little Beach** in Two People's Bay National Park (30km/18 miles east of Albany), a sheltered cove ideal for swimming, and **Two People's Bay** in Manypeaks, a remote swathe of sand accessed via a bushwalk over the headland.

FORESTS AND FRUIT

Turn inland to Mount Barker and veer west via Lake Muir. At Manjimup, join the South Western Highway and head through the apple orchards and forests surrounding **Bridgetown** ⑭, where the **Cidery** (43 Gifford Road; tel: 08-9761 2204; www.thecidery.com.au) offers samples of traditionally crushed and pressed ciders and juices. **Balingup** ⑮ in the Blackwood River Valley, is a lovely spot to bushwalk along part of the Bibbulmun Track (see page 81).

Traverse the underrated **Ferguson Valley** ⑯, an emerging wine region, and stay on the South Western Highway as you pass through Bunbury and go past the lush, fruit-growing area of Donnybrook.

DWELLINGUP

Off the highway to the east is the timber town of **Dwellingup** ⑰, home to the **Hotham Valley Tourist Railway** (tel: 08-9221 4444; www.hothamvalleyrailway.com.au), which operates the Pinjarra Steam Ranger, a steam train to/from Pinjarra, and a weekend excursion to Etmilyn Forest involving a 30-minute bushwalk through blackbutt, jarrah,

red gum and banksia – stunning during wildflower season.

Dwellingup is also home to the **Forest Heritage Centre** (Acacia Street; tel: 08-9538 1395; www.forestdiscoverycentre.com.au; daily 10am–5pm) and a stop on both WA's premier long-distance trails, the Bibbulmun Track (hiking) and the mountain-biker's Munda Biddi Trail (see page 81). Travel back to Perth via the South Western Highway or Kwinana Freeway.

Food and drink

❶ NO ONEFORTY

140 Victoria Street, Bunbury; tel: 08-9721 2254; www.oneforty.com.au; Mon–Fri 7am–4.30pm, Sat 8am–3pm, Sun 8am–2pm; $$
A great spot with a good attitude and menu offering a mix of healthy, homemade and hearty (morning glory burgers for breakfast, bread and butter pudding with ice cream).

❷ BREWHOUSE MARGARET RIVER

5 Bussell Highway, Margaret River; tel: 08-9757 2614; www.brewhousemargaretriver.com.au; Mon–Thu 11am–7pm, Fri–Sun 11am–9pm; $$
Come to Margaret River for the wine, but stay for a beer here at the town's amazing microbrewery, where the restaurant quality food is every bit as lovingly crafted as the ales, and the wood-fired oven is used for far more than just pizza. Loved by locals, it also features regular live music.

Motor Museum of Western Australia

SOUTHERN OCEAN AND GOLDFIELDS

An immense ocean coastline devoid of people, deserts annually flooded by wildflowers, wide-open roads through empty stretches of outback, and gigantic holes in the ground spewing treasure – welcome to the enigmatic Goldfields–Esperance region.

DISTANCE: 1,730km (1,074 miles)
TIME: One week
START/END: Perth
POINTS TO NOTE: Following this route exactly requires a vehicle (see page 130 for info on driving in the outback), but much of it can be done using public transport. Transwa's Prospector train runs daily between Perth and Kalgoorlie (6 hours 45 minutes). Transwa also run coaches to Esperance, and between Esperance and Kalgoorlie. Qantas and Virgin operate regular flights between Perth and Kalgoorlie, and Rex fly to Esperance.

WA covers 2,529,875 sq km (976,790 sq miles). Most of the 2.6-million population hug the coast, almost 2 million of them living in Perth and Fremantle. The immense inland contains properties bigger than many European countries.

The only way to get a true sense of such epic space and distance is to travel the outback on roads where trees, let alone other cars, are rare. When traf-fic does appear it's usually titanic road trains, leaving whirly winds of desert dust in their wake. Empty, on this scale, isn't boring – it's awe-inspiring. Get your play-list sorted and prepare for a road trip.

YORK

Head east from Perth, along the Great Southern Highway, passing through the rural Wheatbelt. Within an hour you'll reach historic **York ❶**. This tiny Avon Valley town is easy to explore on foot: the most impressive build-ings are on Avon Terrace, including the **Motor Museum** (tel: 08-9641 1288; www.yorkmotormuseum.com; daily 9am–4pm), home to over 100 classic and vintage vehicles.

WAVE ROCK

From here it's a two-hour drive to **Hyden ❷**, near iconic **Wave Rock**. (4km/2.5 miles east of town; tel: 08-9880 5052; www.waverock.com.au; $12 per vehicle). Around 15-metres (50ft) high and 110-metres (360ft) long, this unique

Wave Rock   *Coastline of Fitzgerald River National Park*

formation resembles the perfect ocean wave, ripe for surfing, but frozen in time.

The rock is a stunning sight, striped with vertical bands of colour. In spring, orchids and other wildflowers grow around the base in the meagre shade of sheoaks. Nearby are other rock features, including **Hippo's Yawn**, the **Humps** and the **Breakers**. The **Wave Rock Wild Flower Shop and Visitor Centre** (tel: 08-9880 5182; daily 9am–5pm) provides details.

SOUTH COAST

Continue south along State Route 40, passing remote Eastern Wheatbelt set-tlements of Holt Rock and Lake King. At Ravensthorpe, cross the South Coast Highway and keep going until you meet the ocean at **Hopetoun ❸**.

This small settlement borders **Fitzgerald River National Park** (tel: 08-9842 4500; https://parks.dpaw. wa.gov.au/park/fitzgerald-river), one of Australia's most botanically diverse reserves. Almost 20 percent of WA's flora species grow here, some endemic to the park. Wild bushwalking and camping can be enjoyed if you're well equipped, but most roads are unsealed and unsuitable for many vehicles.

Head east, joining the South Coast Highway and passing through **Stokes**

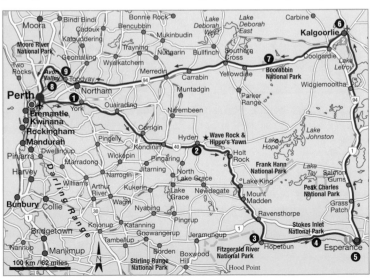

Inlet National Park ④ (https://parks. dpaw.wa.gov.au/park/stokes; camping available), with a picturesque estuary and an abundance of birdlife and bush-walking trails.

SOUTHERN OCEAN

WA's wild southern shore is lonely and evocative, with countless, deserted sandy bays making shapes like teeth marks in the Great Australian Bight. These lead eventually to **Esperance** ❺, hub for an astonishing 500km (311 miles) of coast. With its back to the Pacific, the Esperance region extends across 42,000 sq km (16,216 sq miles), populated by fewer than 15,000 people.

Beside enjoying the town's facilities and restaurants, such as **Fish Face** (see ①), multiple attractions and activities can be organised here, including diving and fishing charters, and boat trips to the area's extraordinary islands, home to myriad marine life. The **Visitor Centre** (corner of Dempster and Kemp streets; tel: 1300 66 44 55/08-9083 1555; www.visitesperance.com; Mon–Fri 9am–5pm, Sat 9am–4pm, Sun 9am–2pm) presents options.

Great Ocean Drive is a 40km (25-mile) DIY route linking beautiful beaches, rocky headlands, steep cliffs and hidden ocean pools. **Rotary** lookout offers a 360-degree view across the Recherche Archipelago, and you can stop for a swim at **Twilight Cove**.

Self-guided trips can be done to the **Wetlands** (7km/4.3 miles north), where almost 100 lakes support 20,000 water birds, and ocean-caressed **Cape Le Grand National Park** (60km/37 miles east) where kangaroos sunbathe on blinding-white sand at **Lucky Bay**.

KALGOORLIE

Head north on Coolgardie-Esperance Highway, the endless road interrupted occasionally by little settlements like Salmon Gums. At a fork just past the goldrush-hangover ghost town of Widgiemooltha, go right to hit Kalgoorlie-Boulder, commonly called **Kalgoorlie** ❻ (www.kalgoorlietourism. com). The wild-west town flowered in the desert after Paddy Hannan struck a rich seam of gold in 1893, triggering a swarm of prospectors and transforming WA's fortunes.

Mining still powers the state, and its epicentre is the **Super Pit** (www.super pit.com.au). This gargantuan open-cut gold mine can be viewed from the **Super Pit lookout** (7am–9pm daily), just off the Goldfields Highway. Night viewing is recommended, with the pit illuminated by high-voltage lights.

Kalgoorlie Tours and Charters (tel: 08-9021 2211; www.kalgoorlietours. com) run regular tours of the pit and the goldfields, and **Kalgoorlie Consolidated Gold Mines** (KCGM) facilitate free tours on the third Sunday of every

Kangaroos at Lucky Bay

month as part of the Kalgoorlie-Boulder Market Day. The one-hour tours depart 9am, 10am and 11am; places available from the Eastern Goldfields Historical Society, Hamilton Street, from 8.30am – first come, first served.

Just north of town, at **Hannans North Tourist Mine** (130 Goldfields Highway, Mullingar; tel: 08-9022 1664; www.hannansnorth.com.au; Sun–Fri 9am–4pm) you can explore a historic shaft, pan for gold and experience modern mining by climbing aboard monster machines (trucks and diggers) and entering an underground refuge chamber, where 12 people can survive for 72 hours.

In its heyday, Kalgoorlie boasted 93 pubs; today 25 remain, and they fall into three categories: drinking dens, family friendly hotels and trendy bars. For something unique, visit **Metropole Hotel** (Burt Street, Boulder), which features a mineshaft leading to the Super Pit. For a beer and a decent feed, try **Paddy's** (see ❷) at the Exchange Hotel.

AVON VALLEY

Return towards Perth along the Great Eastern Highway, via the eucalypt oasis of **Boorabbin National Park** ❼ (tel: 08-9080 5555; https://parks.dpaw. wa.gov.au/park/boorabbin), where diverse wildflowers and woodlands defy WA's harsh environment.

After crossing the Wheatbelt you'll eventually roll into Northam, east-ern gateway to the **Avon Valley** ❽ and home to many historic buildings. The **Visitor Centre** (2 Grey Street; tel: 08-9622 2100; www.northam.wa.gov. au) supplies brochures detailing the Historic Town Walk – a 2km (1-mile) walk and 4km (2.5-mile) drive linking the main interest points. Worth exploring are the **Old Railway Station Museum** (Fitzgerald Street; Sun 10am–4pm) and Australia's longest pedestrian suspension bridge.

Elsewhere in the valley, **Toodyay** ❾ has attractions including Connor's Mill, a working steam-driven flour mill that tells the tale of infamous bushranger Moondyne Joe, son of a Welsh blacksmith transported to Australia for stealing bread.

Food and drink

❶ FISH FACE

1 James Street, Esperance; tel: 08-9071 1601; Tue–Sat 4.30–8.30pm; $$
A deservedly popular place where freshly grilled fish feasts easily transcend the standard flake-and-chip offering.

❷ PADDY'S

135 Hannan Street, Kalgoorlie; tel: 08-9021 2833; www.exchangekalgoorlie.com.au/ paddyseatanddrink; daily 11am–9pm; $$
Good value pub grub in a decent family-friendly dining area within the Exchange Hotel, a historic saloon dating to 1901.

NORTH OF PERTH TO SHARK BAY

Exploring deserts dotted with odd obelisks and beaches made entirely from shells, sandboarding down mountainous dunes, encountering living fossils, dugongs and dolphins – this turquoise coast is an extraordinary adventure.

DISTANCE: 950km (590 miles) one way / 1,768km (1,100 miles) return
TIME: Five days
START: Perth
END: Denham, Shark Bay
POINTS TO NOTE: If possible, do this trip between September and October when blooming wildflowers set the national parks ablaze. Midsummer is scorching. This route requires a vehicle (see page 130 for advice on driving in the outback), but Transwa operate coaches from Perth to Geraldton and Kalbarri, and Rex fly to Monkey Mia several times a week. This route can be combined with Route 15 (Ningaloo Reef and Karijini National Park).

When English ex-pirate-turned-explorer William Dampier sailed into Shark Bay in August 1699, he bequeathed it with a name that could have caused future tourism authorities major migraines. Instead, some super-friendly sea mammals showed up, the area was awarded World Heritage-listing and became one of WA's most-visited destinations, drawing Dampier's compatriots (and travellers from the world over) here in droves.

But there are many more reasons to visit Shark Bay, beyond feeding wild dolphins on a beautiful beach at Monkey Mia, starting with the action-packed attraction-rich cross-country voyage to get there.

LANCELIN

Leave Perth on the Wanneroo Road and hug the Indian Ocean coast through the satellite settlements of Yanchep and Two Rocks, and desolate Moore River National Park, to reach **Lancelin ❶**. The town sits sandwiched between a mighty sandpit and the sea, sheltered by Lancelin and Edwards Islands Nature Reserve. Larger Lancelin Island is home to myriad species of flowers, its own unique lizard and thousands of noisy nesting sea birds.

The crisp white dunes that surround the town are ace for sandboarding (board hire $12.50 for 2.5 hours). The best time to hit the dunes is mid-morn-

Pinnacles Desert in Nambung National Park

ing, when the breeze is lightest. You can also tour the dunes in 4WD vehicles, hire SUP and surfboards, and go dolphin-spotting or fishing. For bookings and more information, see www.lance lin.com.au.

Beachcombing along the apparently endless sand is free and fascinating. The castaway feel of the wild Turquoise Coast was done no harm by the discovery, on a beach near Wedge Island in 2018, of the world's oldest message in a bottle, tossed overboard from a ship in 1886.

NAMBUNG NATIONAL PARK

Follow the Indian Ocean Drive to eerie **Pinnacles Desert ❷**, in the heart of the Nambung National Park (tel: 08-9652 7913; https://parks.dpaw.wa.gov.au/park/nambung).

From the car park and **Pinnacles Desert Discovery Centre** (daily 9.30am–4.30pm), it's a short walk to where stone monuments stand to attention across a sprawling desert, some reaching 3-metres (10ft) high. A circular track leads around the park, with a lookout at the northern end (some tracks aren't suitable for all vehicles, including large campervans.)

Apart from the peculiar Pinnacles, Nambung is also known for beautiful beaches at **Kangaroo Point** and **Hangover Bay**, coastal dune systems and low heathland rich in flowering plants. At the park's northern end, near Cervantes, there's a loop trail and boardwalk at **Lake Thetis** where you can see some fascinating thrombolites (rock-like structures similar to stromatolites, built by micro-organisms).

GREENOUGH

Continue along the Indian Ocean Drive, through the rock-lobster-fishing community of Cervantes and past Jurien Bay. Off to the right is **Lesueur National Park** (tel: 08-9688 6000; https://parks.dpaw.wa.gov.au/park/lesueur), which explodes into a contagion of blooming wildflowers in late winter and spring each year. The park also hosts 122 species of native bird and 52 reptile species, including legless lizards.

Now in WA's Mid-West region, drive through Beekeeper's Nature Reserve (home to 32 registered apiary sites) and Dongara to Greenough, and the **Central Greenough Historical Settlement ❸** (tel: 08-9926 1084; www.nationaltrust.org.au/places/central-greenough; daily 9am–4pm), where you can explore a collection of 19th-century colonial buildings. The 57-km (35-mile) Heritage Trail and Drive (maps available from local tourist offices) is a great way to experience the hamlet and surrounding historical sites.

GERALDTON

Gateway to the north, **Geraldton ❹** is a bustling coastal city with excellent eat-

Nature's Window, Kalbarri National Park

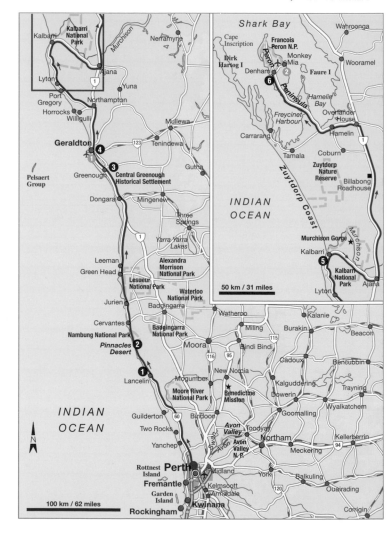

Wildflowers in Geraldton

eries (try **Origin India** – see ❶), ideal as a base for fishing, diving, wildflower-viewing and cultural excursions.

Geraldton Visitors Centre (246 Marine Terrace; tel: 08-9956 6670; www.visitgeraldton.com.au; Mon–Fri 9am–5pm, Sat–Sun 9am–1pm) provides details about guided and DIY adventures, including the 195km (121-mile) **Yamaji Drive Trail**, which visits 14 sites of significance to local Aboriginal people, including the Warglu Trail, Bootenal Spring, Ellendale Pool, Butterabby Graves, Woolya Reserve and Mass Rock.

Explore Geraldton's branch of the **Western Australian Museum** (2 Museum Place, Batavia Coast Marina; tel: 08-9431 8393; www.museum.wa.gov.au; daily 9.30am–3pm; guided highlights tour 11.30am) with displays on the area's history and geology, an aquarium showcasing local marine life, and a Shipwrecks Gallery containing relics from four Dutch vessels that sank off the Batavia Coast, including the *Batavia* herself, plus the *Gilt Dragon, Zuytdorp* and *Zeewijk*.

For a spectacular wildlife experience, visit the **Houtman Abrolhos Islands**, an archipelago of 112 islands 60km (37 miles) west of Geraldton, which seem idyllic now but were lethal to shipping and saw a bloody, awful sequence of events in 1628 (see box). Home to large colonies of marine birds and mammals, the islands offer superb snorkelling, birdwatching and fishing. For multi-day adventures contact **Eco Abrolhos Tours** (tel: 08-9964 5101; www.eco abrolhos.com.au).

KALBARRI NATIONAL PARK

From Geraldton, take the North West Coastal Highway to Northampton, before bearing left on the coast road (Port Gregory Road, then George Grey

Houtman Abrolhos horror story

In 1628, the flagship of the Dutch East India Company, the *Batavia*, weighed anchor and departed on her maiden voyage to the Dutch East Indies. Deliberately sailed off course by the disgruntled skipper, Ariaen Jacobsz, who was planning a mutiny against the company's senior merchant, Francisco Pelsaert, the ship hit the reef near the Abrolhos Islands off the coast of Western Australia.

Pelsaert led a party (including Jacobsz) in a fraught small-boat journey to the mainland in search of water, and then on to Java to seek salvation. Meanwhile, all hell broke loose among the survivors of the wreck, stranded on the island, with a group led by a psychopath called Jeronimus Cornelisz committing mutiny and a massacre, killing at least 110 men, women, and children in what remains Australia's worst mass murder.

Houtman Abrolhos

Drive), past the Pink Lake to reach **Kalbarri ❺**.

Perthites regularly make the six-hour drive to this perennially popular holiday destination and outdoor adventure hub, equipped with snorkel, fishing, surfing and windsurfing gear. The **Visitor Centre** (70 Grey Street; tel: 08-9937 1104; www.kalbarri.org.au; Mon–Sat 9am–5pm, Sun 9am–1pm) has information about activities including charters to view spectacular coastal cliffs and dolphins. Whale-watching cruises are popular June–December when humpbacks gather in the sheltered waters to calve.

Kalbarri is surrounded by rugged **Kalbarri National Park** (tel: 08-9964 0901; https://parks.dpaw.wa.gov.au/park/kalbarri), sliced by 80km (50-mile) Murchison Gorge. Numerous adventure

Hamelin Pool

activities are possible, including canoeing along the Murchison River, abseiling, bushwalking and 4WD tours.

This is a stunning spot to witness displays of wildflowers (in bloom from late July through spring and into early summer), with 21 plant species including banksia, grevillia, kangaroo paw, featherflower, smoke bush, starflower and several orchids that are unique to the area. Sadly the Kalbarri Wild Flower Centre has wilted, but you can stroll an interpretive nature trail or join a guided walk through Kalbarri's Native Botanic Garden.

SHARK BAY MARINE PARK

Rejoin the North West Coastal Highway and head north towards **Denham ❻**, at the heart of WA's first World Heritage-listed area. The **Discovery and Visitor Centre** (53 Knight Terrace; tel: 1300 367 072; www.sharkbayvisit.com.au; Nov–Mar Mon–Fri 9am–4.30pm, Sat–Sun 9am–1pm, Apr–Oct from 10am) has information on activities and attractions, including highlights of **Francois Peron National Park** (tel: 08-9948 2226; https://parks.dpaw.wa.gov.au/park/francois-peron), where red-dirt desert meets azure ocean at **Bottle Bay**.

Half-an-hour south of Denham, **Shell Beach** is one of two beaches on the planet where sand is replaced entirely with shells. Trillions of them, stretching over 100km (62 miles). It's a stunning

Bottlenose Dolphin, Monkey Mia

sight, and the super saline water that laps the shore is genuinely gin clear but so salty it's devoid of all life except for the fragum cockle, source of all the shells which have been used to construct local buildings, including Denham's St Andrews Anglican Church and the Old Pearler Restaurant.

Hamelin Pool, close to the turn-off from the highway, is home to stromatolites. Boardwalks take visitors close to these single-celled photosynthesizing microbes, which are the oldest form of life on Earth – 'living fossils' of our very, very far-distant relatives.

Dirk Hartog Island (www.dirkhartog island.com), offers scuba diving, sightings of dugongs, whales and turtles, and opportunities to learn about the art and culture of the traditional inhabitants of the Coral Coast, during walking, kayaking and 4WD routes led by **Wula Gura Eco Cultural Adventures** (tel: 0429 708 847/0432 029 436; www. wulagura.com.au).

MONKEY MIA

Most people, however, will rush to magical **Monkey Mia**, where a group of bottlenose dolphins has been visiting the beach to interact with humans for over 40 years, across several generations (interestingly, only female adults and calves come in). The animals are wild, and the timing of their visits varies, but they usually come close to the shore up to three times a day, most frequently in the morning. It's possible to stand shin-deep in the water and feed them (under the supervision of park rangers), but you can't swim with the dolphins. **Boughshed Restaurant** (see ②) is a good place to stop for a light bite.

You are now 850km (528 miles) north of Perth. Either head back along the North West Coastal Highway, or continue north towards Coral Bay and Exmouth to link up with Route 15: Ningaloo Reef and Outback WA.

Food and drink

① ORIGIN INDIA

60 Chapman Road, Geraldton; tel: 08-9904 7244; www.originindia.com.au; daily 11.30am–2pm and 4.30–9.30pm; $$
One of the most raved about Indian restaurants in WA, with friendly service and fragrant, spicy and aromatic offerings – give the goat curry a go.

② BOUGHSHED RESTAURANT

1 Monkey Mia Road; tel: 08-9948 1171; https://parksandresorts.rac.com.au/monkey-mia; daily 7am to late; $$$
Part of the RAC Monkey Mia Dolphin Resort, which monopolises the destination, this fancy restaurant twins stunning views of Shark Bay with a menu full of regional ingredients given an international twist, such as crocodile-and-prawn Tom Kha Kai, and linguini made with Shark Bay blue swimmer crab.

Gascoyne River

NINGALOO AND THE PILBARA

Snorkel out to a spectacular coral reef from deserted golden beaches, swim with manta rays and whale sharks, traverse a rusty red landscape punctuated by parks populated by fantastic beasts, and discover ancient cultures.

DISTANCE: 3,833km (2,382 miles)
TIME: One week
START/END: Perth
POINTS TO NOTE: This route can be done as a stand-alone adventure to the tropical north coast and inland area, or combined with Route 14 and/or Route 16. Either way, a vehicle is required to follow it faithfully. See page 130 for advice on driving in the Outback. If time is short, Rex operates flights to Carnarvon, and Qantas and Virgin fly to Port Hedland. Time your trip between late May and August to swim with whale sharks.

It's not every day you get the chance to meet the planet's biggest fish and oldest culture in one trip, but this escapade combines Ningaloo Reef encounters with an adventure though the immense ruddy inland of Western Australia's Pilbara and Mid-West regions, populated by people for millennia.

CARNAVON

Sitting just below the Tropic of Capricorn, on the banks of the beautiful Gascoyne River, **Carnarvon ❶** is the gateway to the northern Coral Coast. The **Visitor Centre** (21 Robinson Street; tel: 08-9941 1146; www.carnarvon.org.au; Mon–Fri 9am–4.30pm, Sat 9am–noon), has information about local experiences, including fishing from One-Mile Jetty (a 1,493-metre/4,898ft wooden structure dating to 1897), taking the tramway and exploring Gwoonwardu Mia Aboriginal Cultural Centre, which celebrates the five Indigenous language groups of the Gascoyne region, and features an art gallery.

The **Space and Technology Museum** (Mahoney Avenue; tel: 08-9941 9901; www.carnarvonmuseum.org.au; daily 10am–2pm, Apr–Sep until 3pm), opened by Buzz Aldrin in 2012, focusses on Carnarvon Tracking Station and the OTC Satellite Earth Station, which both played historical roles in early space exploration. The Tracking Station 10km (6 miles) south of Carnarvon supported NASA's Gemini, Apollo and Skylab pro-

OTC Satellite Earth Station   *Strolling along a beautiful beach near Ningaloo reef*

grammes 1964–75, employing 220 people, and was the last station to communicate with space capsules leaving Earth's orbit, and the last to make contact before splashdown in the Pacific. The OTC Satellite Earth Station, which houses the museum, features the 12.8-metre (42ft) wide Casshorn antenna, which relayed Neil Armstrong's first steps on the Moon from NASA's Honeysuckle Creek Tracking Station on 21 July 1969, the day of the Apollo 11 moon landing.

AROUND LAKE MACLEOD

Picturesque Pelican Point is good for swimming, and massive Miaboolya Beach just north of the river is worth a look. Further north, west of landlocked Lake MacLeod, a spectacular coastline unfolds, with blowholes, sheltered beaches and wild seascapes where whales can be seen during their annual migration June–November. Point Quobba, a calm coral-filled lagoon ringed by sandy white beaches, is ideal for snorkelling and swimming.

Red Bluff, on Quobba Station, at the southern end of the Ningaloo Reef Marine Park, is a genuine outback working station. Another working station, Gnaraloo (www.gnaraloo.com), is a major breeding area for endangered loggerhead turtles. From November to late January, loggerhead, hawksbill and green turtles lay eggs on local beaches, and Gnaraloo hosts a Turtle Conservation Program in which visitors can participate.

Keep trucking on the North West Coastal Highway, around the eastern bank of Lake MacLeod, and past signs announcing your arrival into the Tropic of Capricorn.

NINGALOO

Continue to **Coral Bay**, a town that nestles tight into Ningaloo, with Australia's only fringing reef – meaning the coral starts right at the water's edge, making it accessible to everyone, including children. Over 500 different species of fish are resident or regular visitors to the reef here. Further out, whale sharks, manta rays and loggerhead turtles are encountered. You can arrange boat trips to swim with mighty manta rays with operators from Coral Bay, including **Ningaloo Marine Interactions** (tel: 08 9948 5190; www.mantaraycoralbay.com.au).

On trips departing from **Exmouth ②** it's possible to snorkel with the biggest fish on the planet: the whale shark, which can grow to 10 metres (33 feet). Charters sail daily during the late-May–August season. Companies operating tours include Ningaloo Whalesharks (tel: 1800 994 210/08-9949 4777; www.ningaloo haLesharks.com). Humpback whale sightings are common too. For experienced bubble blowers, **Exmouth Navy Pier** is regarded as one of Australia's top 10 dive sites, and one of the world's best shore dives. Dive Ningaloo (www.diveningaloo. com.au) hold the license. **Whalers Restaurant** (see ①) is a nice spot for seafood.

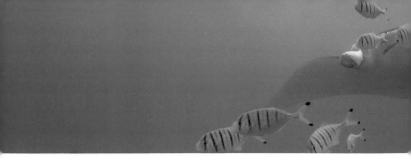

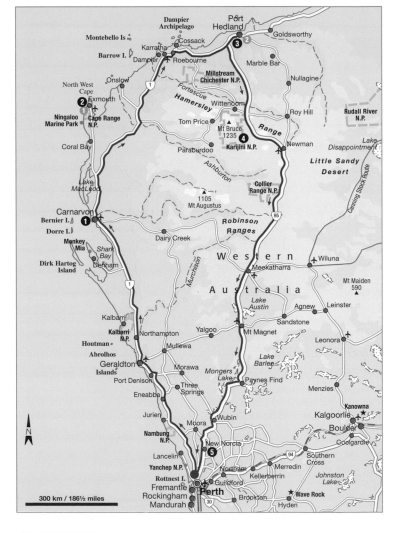

Dampier
Archipelago

Port
Hedland

Montebello Is

Karratha   Cossack   Goldsworthy

3   **2**

Barrow I.

Dampier   Roebourne   Marble Bar

North West   Onslow   Nullagine

Cape

**Millstream
Chichester N.P.**

2 Exmouth   *Fortescue*   Wittenoom

**Ningaloo
Marine Park**   **Cape Range
N.P.**   **Hamersley**   Roy Hill   **Rudall River
N.P.**

Tom Price   *Range*

Coral Bay   Mt Bruce
1235 ▲   **Karijini N.P.**   Newman   *Lake
Disappointment*

Paraburdoo   **4**

*Little Sandy
Desert*

*Lake
MacLeod*   *Ashburton*   **Collier
Range N.P.**

▲ 1105
Mt Augustus   *Canning Stock Route*

Carnarvon   *Robinson
Ranges*

Bernier I.   **1**   95

Dorre I.   Dairy Creek   *W e s t e r n*

**Monkey
Mia**   *Shark
Bay*   Wiluna

Denham   *Murchison*   Meekatharra   Mt Maiden
590 ▲

**Dirk Hartog
Island**   *A u s t r a l i a*

*Lake
Austin*   Agnew   Leinster

Sandstone

Kalbarri   Yalgoo   Mt Magnet   Leonora

**Kalbarri
N.P.**   Northampton   *Lake
Barlee*

Houtman   Mullewa

Abrolhos   Morawa   Menzies

Geraldton   *Mongers
Lake*

Islands   Port Denison   Three   Paynes Find   Kanowna
Springs   Kalgoorlie ★

Eneabba   Wubin   Boulder

Jurien   Moora   Coolgardie

**Nambung
N.P.**   New Norcia   Southern
Cross   *Johnston
Lake*

Lancelin   **5**   94

Yanchep N.P.   Northam   Merredin

Rottnest I.   Guildford   Kellerberrin   ★ **Wave Rock**

Fremantle   **Perth**   Brookton

Rockingham   30   Hyden

Mandurah

N

300 km / 186½ miles

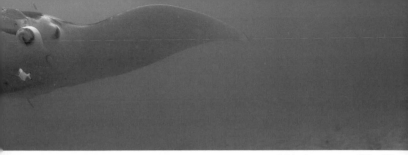

Majestic manta ray off Coral Bay

Southwest of Exmouth, spread along a rugged, dry limestone ridge, is **Cape Range National Park** (tel: 08-9949 2808; https://parks.dpaw.wa.gov.au/park/cape-range). Boat trips through the sheer cliffs of **Yardie Creek Gorge** are popular, with reliable sightings of black-footed rock wallabies. From the foot of the range, it's possible to peruse beautiful beaches, waters and coral gardens. Turquoise Bay is noted for translucent water and white-sand beaches. Snorkelling on the inside of the reef is possible from the shore here, with hundreds of fish, ray and turtle species for company.

PILBARA COAST

Amid the spinifex-covered plains of Cane River Conservation Park, a turning left leads to **Onslow**, where the sun rises and sets over water and trips to the fishing and diving destination of the Mackerel Islands depart.

Carry on to **Karratha**, where modern mining meets ancient culture in Ngarluma Country. The Visitor Centre (tel: 08-9144 4600; www.karrathavisitorcentre.com.au; Mon–Fri 9am–4pm, Sat–Sun 9am–1pm) explains how to learn about Aboriginal culture on the Yaburara Heritage Trail, which features rock art, middens and artefacts. Activities include mountain biking, kitesurfing, paddleboarding and bird watching.

Dampier is the departure point for cruises to the spectacular Dampier Archipelago. Look out for the Red Dog memorial, and follow the Red Dog Trail dedicated to the antics of a local canine character (see page 139). Some 120km (75 miles) offshore from here are the Montebello Islands, which would have been an idyllic destination if the British hadn't conducted three nuclear explosions there in 1952 and 1956.

Nearby **Hearson's Cove** is a good spot to get a glimpse of the Staircase to the Moon (visible when a full moon rises over mudflats). Settlers Beach at the ghost town of **Cossack**, just around the coast, is another excellent place to witness this phenomenon.

Port Hedland ❸, the Pilbara's main town, rich in mining and indigenous history and with a large working harbour, has a Staircase to the Moon viewing

Ningaloo Marine Park

Ningaloo Reef – Australia's largest coral reef, with 250 species of coral and more than 500 fish types – is protected by a marine park that stretches 260km (160 miles) from Amherst Point around North West Cape into the Exmouth Gulf. Western Ningaloo is an unspoilt delight for divers. Coral outcrops can be reached just 20 metres (65ft) from the beach, though they extend 7km (4.5 miles) into the ocean. Dolphins, dugongs, manta rays, giant cod and sharks abound. Whale sharks visit the reef from March to August, and swimming with them has become a large industry operating out of Exmouth.

Dales Gorge, Karijini

deck. The **Visitor Centre** (13 Wedge Street; tel: 08-9173 1711; www.visit porthedland.com; Mon–Fri 9am–5pm) has details of tours and attractions, including trips to Marble Bar, known as Australia's hottest town and named after a local feature that turned out to be made from jasper, not marble. **Pilbara Room** (see ❷) is a great stop here for breakfast or dinner.

Food and drink

❶ WHALERS RESTAURANT

2 Murat Road, Exmouth; tel: 08-9949 2416; www.whalersrestaurant.com.au; daily 5.30pm–10pm; $$$$

Family run restaurant in Exmouth Escape Resort, which features good seafood cooked to perfection from locally sourced fruits de mer. Give the seafood medley for two a spin. A tasty vegan option is available.

❷ PILBARA ROOM

Corner of Sutherland Street, Port Hedland; tel: 08-9173 1044; www.porthedland. wa.hospitalityinns.com.au; daily breakfast (6:30am–9am) and dinner (6pm–8:30pm); $$$

A side street surprise (within the Hospitality Motel) that exceeds expectations with a wide-ranging menu offering good-quality pasta, seafood and vegetarian dishes, a decent wine list (and cocktails) and delicious desserts.

KARIJINI

Turn inland, traversing the great red expanse of the Pilbara proper, to visit WA's second largest park, **Karijini** ❹ (visitor centre just off Banjima Drive; tel: 08-9189 8121; https://parks.dpaw. wa.gov.au/park/karijini; daily Feb–Nov 9am–4pm), traditional home to the Banyjima, Kurrama and Innawonga Aboriginal people. The stunning pink plateau here is interrupted by red mountains, escarpments, valleys and gorges. Don't miss Dales Gorge, Fortescue Falls, Weano Gorge and Oxers Lookout.

In case you're wondering, *this* is where to find fantastic beasts, including dragons, thorny devils, legless lizards, pythons, kangaroos, rock-wallabies, echidnas and several bat species. Also look out for large pebble cairns (50cm/19.5 inches high and covering up to 9 sq metres/97 sq ft) built by the industrious 60mm (2.4in) -long western pebble-mound mouse.

It's over 1,420km (882 miles) back to Perth along the Great Northern Highway from Karijini, with leg-stretching breaks in the gold-mining towns of Meekatharra and Mount Magnet.

Much closer to Perth, and in stark contrast to dusty Outback, is the Benedictine community of **New Norcia** ❺, founded by Dom Rosendo Salvado in 1846. The Heritage Trail links the main sites, including a museum and art gallery, and goes via the bakery, which serves tasty New Norcia nut cake and Dom Salvado Pan Chocolatti.

Along the coastal route to Port Hedland

BROOME AND THE KIMBERLEY

Travel Western Australia's other-worldly tropical Top End, from the foot of the Staircase to the Moon in Broome to the Mars-like red bumps of the Bungle Bungle Range in the Kimberley, via deep gorges and meteor craters.

DISTANCE: 3,414km (2,121 miles) one way

TIME: One week

START: Perth

END: Wyndham

POINTS TO NOTE: This route requires the use of a vehicle (see page 130 for tips on driving in the Outback), although if time is tight Qantas and Virgin fly between Perth and Broome. It can be combined with Routes 14 and 15, or done as a standalone adventure. You can return to Perth or continue into the Northern Territory towards Darwin. Spring brings wildflowers and the Staircase to the Moon phenomenon, but avoid the worst of the Wet and cyclone season: November–April. Note: when travelling across Aboriginal land, respect for the culture, privacy and people is paramount.

Urbane, polite Perth is a long way from pearl-farming Broome and the epic environment of the Kimberley, in terms of distance and culture. Here casual conversations can be about crocs or coffee, and people go flight-seeing instead of sightseeing.

If you have time to explore, take the coast-hugging route from Perth via the parks, settlements and resorts that shadow Shark Bay (see page 96) and the Ningaloo Reef-facing parts of the Pilbara (see page 101). Otherwise, sort out some good road trip tunes and do the last section of Route 15 in reverse, travelling 1,600km (994 miles) to Port Hedland on the Great Northern Highway.

BROOME

From Port Hedland (see page 101), head east along the arched coast called Eighty Mile Reach to **Broome ❶**. The **Visitor Centre** (1 Hamersley Street; tel: 08-9195 2200; www.visitbroome.com.au; Mon–Fri 8.30am–4pm, Sat–Sun 9am–noon) provides information on attractions and activities, ranging from pearl tours and camel rides to indigenous cultural experiences and flight-seeing trips to the famous Horizontal Falls on the far north coast.

Camel ride on Cable Beach

The website publishes dates for the 'Staircase to the Moon' phenomenon, an optical illusion created when moon-light reflects on the flats of Roebuck Bay during low-water spring tides, celebrated with night markets where all sorts of food and drink is available.

A sunset camel ride along **Cable Beach**, a 22km (14-mile) stretch of white sand, is a memorable experience; the **Zoo Keeper's Store** (see ❶) is a great place to refuel. Native animals can be viewed at the popular **Malcolm Douglas Crocodile Park and Animal Refuge** (Broome Road; tel: 08-9193 6580; www.malcolmdouglas.com.au; daily 2–5pm) – feeding time for the crocs is 3pm. At various points around this coast, giant dinosaur tracks, thought to be 130-million-years old, can be viewed (see www.dinosaurcoast.org.au for more).

CAPE LEVEQUE

If you have a 4WD and a sense of adventure, a road trip from Broome to Cape Leveque, traversing the Dampier Peninsula, is amazing. Parts of the Cape Leveque Road remain unsealed, very sandy and badly corrugated, however, and can be impassable for standard vehicles. Always check conditions before setting off.

At **Beagle Bay** the Sacred Heart Church has a beautiful altar decorated with mother-of-pearl, while **Middle Lagoon** (www.middlelagoon.com.au) offers great fishing, safe swimming, camping, beach shelters and self-contained log cabins. **Lombadina** (tel: 08-9192 4936; www.lombadina.com) is an Aboriginal commu-

Pearls

During the 1920s, Broome was the capital of the planet's pearling industry, with more than 300 luggers (pearling vessels) competing for finds off the northwest coast. Most of the divers were Japanese, for whom the real wealth lay in the mother-of-pearl shell, which was used in jewellery and for buttons (a pearl was an unexpected bonus). It was a dangerous job, as the Japanese Cemetery testifies.

Broome suffered a crash when plastic buttons flooded the market after World War II. The recent development of cultured pearls has revitalised the industry (although the harvesting now occurs in remote aquatic farms), and several Broome jewellery shops, including one owned by the dominant pearling operator, Paspaley Pearls (www.paspaley.com), sell fine pearls in a variety of settings.

With a strong Aboriginal culture and large Asian population, Broome has retained plenty of character, apparent during a stroll through the timber dwellings of Chinatown, with its multilingual street signs. The town comes alive each August/September, when fishermen, farmers, miners, drovers and tourists swell the population tenfold for **Shinju Matsuri** – Festival of the Pearl (www.shinjumatsuri.com.au).

Cruising along dirt roads near Cape Leveque

nity offering accommodation and tours from a stunning beach. **One Arm Point** (aka Ardyaloon; tel: 08-9192 4932) is another welcoming community where you

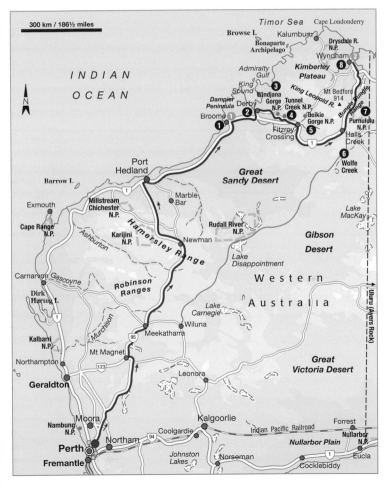

can visit an aquaculture hatchery breeding juvenile trochus shells.

DERBY

Around 216km (134 miles) northeast is **Derby** ❷, epicentre of West Kimberley's huge cattle-producing region. From here, sightseeing is mostly done by light plane, to places such as **King Sound** and the **Buccaneer Archipelago** – experiences that reveal one of the world's most spectacularly beautiful coastlines, a maze of islands, red cliffs and white beaches, uninhabited except for the mining communities of Cockatoo Island and Koolan Island.

Some 7km (4.5 miles) outside Derby is a stout boab tree reputed to have been used as an overnight prison for prisoners being transported during colonial times. The boab (a close relation of the southern African baobab tree) is often known as the 'bottle tree' and can have a circumference greater than its height – the girth of this one exceeds 14 metres (46ft).

GORGES

To the north of the sealed Great Northern Highway are several gorgeous gorges, which may not be accessible at certain times and in some vehicles due to the state of unsealed roads after heavy weather.

Windjana Gorge National Park ❸ (tel: 08-9195 5500; https://parks.dpaw. wa.gov.au/park/windjana-gorge; open during the dry season only, Apr–Nov) on the Lennard River has good walking and camping. This is a spiritual place for the Bunuba, who believe powerful creation spirits called Wandjina reside here. Aboriginal guerrilla leader Jandamarra, who led an organised armed insurrection against European colonisation, used the gorge as a hideout, and was wounded at Pigeon's Rock during a gun battle in 1894.

In **Tunnel Creek National Park** ❹ (tel: 08-9195 5500; https://parks. dpaw.wa.gov.au/park/tunnel-creek; dry season only), you can walk through an underground stream course populated by bats. This cave system was another hideout for Jandamarra, who was killed outside its entrance in 1897, after being hunted down by an indigenous tracker called Micki, whose children were being held by authorities.

East of Derby, on the Fitzroy River near the township of Fitzroy Crossing, is **Geikie Gorge** ❺ (tel: 08-9191 5112; https://parks.dpaw.wa.gov.au/park/danggu-geikie-gorge; dry season only). At 14km (9 miles) long, with limestone cliffs up to 30 metres (100ft) high, this is one of the northwest's most spectacular gorges and a cracking camping spot. Boat tours (May–Oct; see website for bookings) take place along the river, where freshwater crocodiles sunbake at the water's edge and flying-foxes, sea eagles and rare purple-crowned fairy-wrens flit through the air. Below you can see sawfish and stingrays that have adapted to life in fresh water. Interesting boat tours conducted by Aboriginal rangers (call 0417 907 609/08-9191

Wandjina paintings

5355 to book tickets) also take place, explaining their connection to the land.

The Great Northern Highway cuts along the southern perimeter of the Kimberley before entering the modern township of **Halls Creek**, with its comfortable hotels and air-conditioned supermarkets. At Old Halls Creek, remnants of the 1884 gold rush can be seen. Around 130km (80 miles) south of Halls Creek is the **Wolfe Creek** ❻ meteorite crater, the world's second largest.

PURNULULU NATIONAL PARK

The turn-off 110km (68 miles) north of Halls Creek leads to a 4WD track to one of the most astonishing natural features in the world: the **Bungle Bungle Range** ❼. The Bungles cover some 640 sq km (247 sq miles) of the Ord River Valley with a labyrinth of orange and black (caused by the black lichen and orange silica) horizontally tiger-striped, domed mountains. Within the canyons and gorges of the **Purnululu National Park** are palm-filled grottoes, enormous caves and white-sand beaches. The rough track from the highway deters many, so a thriving industry has arisen in Kununurra to fly tourists over (and, more recently, into) the Bungle Bungles.

A true gem of the Kimberley lies to the north of Purnululu: Argyle Diamond Mine, owned by Rio Tinto, is the world's largest, extracting some 1,000kg (6.5 tons) of diamonds each year. The Argyle Diamond Pipe was discovered in 1979 and remains the only source of deep-pink diamonds. Air tours to the mine are available from Kununurra.

WYNDHAM

The most northerly port in Western Australia, Wyndham is a small, scattered community that has changed little since the days of the gold rush. You can see large crocodiles lying on the mudflats below the Wyndham wharf; cattle that miss their footing when being loaded onto ships provide an occasional meal. Stop by the **Croc Café and Bakery** (see ❷) here for classic Aussie light bites.

Food and drink

❶ ZOO KEEPER'S STORE

2 Challenor Drive, Broome; tel: 08-9192 0015; Thu–Mon 7am–noon and 5.30–9pm; $$$
Brilliant breakfasts and delicious dinners made from gourmet and local produce. A top spot to simply sit and sip a coffee, long juice or beer by Cable Beach Resort.

❷ CROC CAFÉ AND BAKERY

12 Great Northern Highway, Wyndham; tel: 0457 826 616; Mon–Sat 7am–2pm; $
You're not exactly spoilt for choice in Wyndham, but you don't need too many options when the crocodile and barramundi pies are this good. Finish off with a lovely lamington – it doesn't get more Aussie than this.

DIRECTORY

Hand-picked hotels and restaurants to suit all budgets and tastes, organised by area, plus select nightlife listings, an alphabetical listing of practical information and an overview of the best books and films to give you a flavour of the region.

Accommodation   110

Restaurants   118

Nightlife   126

A–Z   128

Books and film   138

Duxton Hotel, Perth

ACCOMMODATION

Perth, Fremantle and most popular destinations across Western Australia have a wide range of accommodation options, and you're unlikely to have difficulty finding a place to stay unless there is a major event in progress. Generally speaking, standards are good and high-quality, clean accommodation is available in all price ranges.

Perth City Centre

All Suites Hotel

12 Victoria Avenue; tel: 08-9318 4444; www.allsuitesperth.com.au; $$

A range of modern apartments, with rooftop spa and barbecue area, very near the CBD and Adelaide Terrace, and within walking distance of the river and shops. Each apartment is equipped with a kitchen, fridge, clothes washer, as well as Cable TV and Wi-Fi.

Central Caravan Park

34 Central Avenue, Ascot; tel: 08-9277 1704; www.perthcentral.com.au; $

Situated just 7km (4.5 miles) from the city centre, this park near the river has

> Price for a double room for one night without breakfast:
> $$$$ = over A$220
> $$$ = A$150–220
> $$ = A$80–150
> $ = below A$80

powered sites, tent sites, glamping sites, 1-bed cabins and 2-bed park homes; plus a heated pool, barbecues and a campers' kitchen. Linen is included. Buses to Perth run every 30 minutes.

Criterion Hotel Perth

560 Hay Street; tel: 08-9325 5155; www.criterion-hotel-perth.com.au; $$

An old-school hotel in a beautifully restored Art Deco building, positioned in a great central location (opposite historic Perth Town Hall and close to shopping arcades, Kings Park, Elizabeth Quay), offering no-frills accommodation.

Duxton Hotel Perth

1 St George's Terrace; tel: 08-9261 8000/1800 681 118; www.perth.duxtonhotels.com; $$$

Sleeping in an old tax office might not top your bucket list, but this beautifully renovated hotel in a centrally located heritage building is a lovely luxury option. There's free Wi-Fi, a restaurant and club lounge, gym, sauna and steam room, and an outdoor heated pool with hot tub surrounded by a private courtyard.

Hyatt Regency Perth

99 Adelaide Terrace; tel: 08-9225 1234; www.hyatt.com; $$$

With a 19-metre heated pool and views over the Swan River, plus a tennis court, fitness centre and sauna, the Hyatt has

everything expected of a 5-star hotel. Elegant dining or café-style quaffing is available in several bars and restaurants. Between the CBD and East Perth, it's close to shopping and entertainment options.

Pan Pacific Perth

207 Adelaide Terrace, tel: 08-9224 7777; www.panpacific.com; $$$
A luxury hotel in the heart of the action, with 486 rooms, many with views over the Swan and city. With a swimming pool and various eating options, it's a short walk from Elizabeth Quay and close to the city's main retail, dining and entertainment precincts.

Quest West End

451 Murray Street, tel: 08-9480 3888; www.questapartments.com.au; $$$
Offering serviced-apartment style hotel rooms, Quest West End is located in the heart of Perth's CBD, a short walk from Perth Arena, Perth Convention and Exhibition Centre, His Majesty's Theatre, and Kings Square Precinct. There are 35 serviced units, including one- and two-bedroom apartments perfect for families.

Ramada Perth, The Outram

32 Outram Street, West Perth; tel: 08-9322 4888; www.wyndhamhotels.com; $$$
A boutique hotel centrally located roughly equidistant from Kings Park, the CBD, Subiaco and Northbridge, the stylish Outram offers the option of hotel rooms or chic two-bedroom apartments with fully equipped kitchens, for those who would rather semi self-cater. The on-site café offers a reasonably priced breakfast.

Sullivans Hotel

166 Mounts Bay Road; tel: 08-9321 8022; www.sullivans.com.au; $$
A small, friendly, family-owned hotel on the river below Kings Park escarpment, near Jacobs Ladder, which goes the extra distance to make guests feel at home. Free internet access and parking, with a free Blue CAT bus running into town from outside. Boasts a café, bar, private garden and swimming pool.

East and South Perth

Broadwater Resort Apartments

137 Melville Parade, Como; tel: 08-9474 4222; www.broadwaters.com.au; $$
One-, two- and three-bedroom luxury apartments, situated south of the river, close to Perth Zoo and restaurants. Features include a swimming pool, spa and tennis court, and alfresco courtyard. Apartments have full kitchen.

Crown Perth

Burswood, East Perth; tel: 1800 556 688; www.crownperth.com.au/hotels; $$$$
This modern casino-focused resort by the Swan has three hotels in among its 32 restaurants and bars, nightclub, recreational facilities and assorted gambling dens: the 397-room Metropol, 291-room Promenade and 500-room luxury hotel Crown Towers. They feature all the trimmings you'd expect (pools, saunas and so on).

Durham Lodge

165 Shepperton Road, Victoria Park; tel: 08-9361 8000; www.durhamlodge.com; $$$

A chic, boutique B&B in an elegant old home in Victoria Park, south of the river, close to attractions such as the zoo and Perth Stadium. Features include a baby grand piano, comfortable furnishings, private guest wing and rooms with spa bath/shower, TV, bar and fridge.

Regal Apartments

11 Regal Place; tel: 08-9221 8614; www. regalapartments.com.au; $$

Apartments that sleep up to seven, with fully equipped kitchen and laundry. Positioned amid restaurants, cafés and bars, close to Claisebrook Cove and Perth Stadium, and 5-minutes' walk from Claisebrook railway station. Free CAT bus to the city.

Northbridge and Subiaco

Best Western Northbridge Apartments

228 James Street; tel: 08-9227 2888; www. bestwestern.com; $$

Two and three-bedroom fully-furnished modern apartments, centrally located in Northbridge, home to Perth's art gallery and a rich mix of cafés, bars, nightclubs, markets and restaurants. Features include a pool and free Wi-Fi.

Billabong Backpackers Resort

381 Beaufort Street; tel: 08-9328 7720; www.billabongresort.com.au; $

Next to Northbridge's entertainment and restaurant area, this budget option offers backpackers the choice of dorms, private rooms and deluxe doubles. With a pool and gym, weekly rates of $150, and $5 meals available every night, it's hard to argue with the value.

The Emperor's Crown

85 Stirling Street; tel: 08-9227 1400; www. emperorscrown.com.au; $

A good example of modern, high-quality budget accommodation, the clean and simple Emperors Crown is just 5 minutes' walk from Perth CBD and the nightlife of Northbridge. Various accommodation types are available, from dorms to private rooms.

The Witch's Hat

148 Palmerston Street; tel: 08-9228 4228; www.witchs-hat.com; $

Off Russell Square, Northbridge, in a historic 1897 town house, this is a very pleasant, popular, cheerful and characterful modern backpackers hostel, which puts on events and parties for guests and takes hospitality seriously.

Fremantle

Be. Fremantle Apartments

43 Mews Road, Challenger Harbour; tel: 08-9430 3888; www.befremantle.com.au; $$$

Split-level apartments here have harbour or marina views; studio, 1-, 2- and 3-bed apartments are available. Choose from open-plan or townhouse layouts. Features include fully equipped

kitchen, laundry facilities and a spacious living/dining area.

Hamptons Inn Bed & Breakfast

34 Hampton Road; tel: 0424 063 457;
www.hamptonsinn.com.au; $$$

Choose from four spacious bedrooms, all en suite (three with spas), featuring king or queen-sized beds, in a restored heritage-listed, single-level cottage (1913), with a library. Free Wi-Fi and freshly brewed espresso coffee.

Hougoumont Hotel, Fremantle

15 Bannister Street; tel: 08-6117 2540;
www.hougoumonthotel.com; $$$

A unique, boutique small-room hotel (double-size rooms available) made from shipping containers. Offers complimentary simple breakfast, plus free cheeses and wines in the lounge in late afternoon. Located right beside Cappuccino Strip and a short stroll to Fremantle Prison and the markets.

Port Mill Bed and Breakfast

3/17 Essex Street; tel: 08-9433 3832 www.portmillbb.com.au; $$

A boutique B&B, with four deluxe and beautifully appointed rooms, all en suite, in a heritage building (a flour mill built in 1862) in the heart of Fremantle. Some boast a balcony. Free Wi-Fi.

Beaches

Cottesloe Beach Chalets

6 John Street; tel: 08-9383 5000; https://cottesloebeachchalets.com.au; $$

In an excellent position, just off oceanfront Marine Parade, these no-frills self-contained chalets sleep up to 5. They have cooking facilities, laundry, pool and barbecue. Close to the pub. Popular with younger visitors.

Dunes Scarborough Beach

15 Filburn Street; tel: 08-9245 2797; www.perthdunes.com; $$

Set back from the West Coast Highway, but close to the beach and facilities, and 20 minutes from Fremantle, these modern, well-appointed two-bed units have kitchens, laundry and a private courtyard with barbecue. Minimum stay often applies.

Rendezvous Observation City Hotel

The Esplanade; tel: 08-9245 1000; www.rendezvoushotels.com; $$

A luxury hotel on the beach, overlooking the Indian Ocean. This rare example of a high-rise building on Perth's coast has facilities including several restaurants and bars, nightclub, pool, spa, tennis courts and gym.

Rosemoore Cottage

2 Winifred Street, Mosman Park; tel: 08-9384 8214; www.rosemoore.com.au; $$

Between North Fremantle and Cottesloe beaches in Mosman, this B&B offers comfortable accommodation in a renovated house with country-style furnishings, walking distance from the railway station and bus services, and two minutes' drive from the ocean.

The restaurant and bar at Hotel Rottnest

Rottnest Island

Discovery Rottnest Island

Pinky Beach; tel: 08-6350 6170; www.discoveryholidayparks.com.au/discovery-rottnest-island; $$$$

Opened in March 2019, and tucked in behind the dunes of Pinky Beach, this facility offers super glamping accommodation in 83 eco-tents, with even the base option including private en suites and outdoor decks, and the premium eco-luxe option featuring superb sea views.

Hotel Rottnest

1 Bedford Avenue; tel: 08-9292 5011; www.hotelrottnest.com.au; $$$

Resort-style accommodation in a 4-star hotel featuring bayside rooms with private courtyards that overlook the majestic Thompson Bay. The hotel restaurant offers great food.

Rottnest Campground

Near the Basin; tel: 08-9432 9111; www.rottnestisland.com; $

Sleep under the stars in one of 43 non-powered, sand-covered sites between the main settlement and the beach at the Basin. There's an ablution block and a communal camp kitchen, with cooking facilities including barbecues.

Swan Valley and Perth Hills

Mundaring Weir Hotel

Mundaring Weir Road, Mundaring; tel: 08-9295 1106; www.mundaringweirhotel.com.au; $$

An historic hotel surrounded by jarrah forest, very popular with walkers using the many local trails. Eleven modern units overlook the forest, or pool/amphitheatre area, where open-air concerts are held in the summer months and kangaroos roam around in the evenings. Rooms have open wood fires and good facilities.

The Rose & Crown Hotel

105 Swan Street, Guildford; tel: 08-9347 8100; www.rosecrown.com.au; $$

Situated in green Guildford, gateway to the vineyards of the Swan Valley, this historic hotel (WA's oldest, built in 1841) is recognised by the National Trust as a significant landmark. The hotel has 28 motel units in its lodge and four boutique rooms. Good food too.

South of Perth

Armadale Cottage Bed & Breakfast

3161 Albany Highway, Armadale; tel: 08-9497 1663; www.armadalecottage.com.au; $$$

A friendly, classy, 5-star, attractive AAA-Rated B&B in the foothills of Perth. All rooms are spacious, en suite and have a private entrance. A full breakfast is included.

Atrium Hotel

65 Ormsby Terrace, Mandurah; tel: 08-9535 6633; www.atriumhotel.com.au; $$

Within walking distance of the beach, this hotel is centred on an impressive atrium with palm-fringed, heated indoor pool and spa, cocktail bar and

The Rose & Crown Hotel

restaurant. Accommodation comprises studios, one-, two- and three-bed apartments with full cooking facilities. There's also a sauna, tennis, and games room.

Mandurah Foreshore Motel

2 Gibson Street, Mandurah; tel: 08-9535 5577; www.foreshoremotel.com.au; $$

Excellent value here, with 18 doubles and a selection of family rooms (all en suite) situated in the centre of Mandurah, close to restaurants and shops, and facing the foreshore. Facilities include a swimming pool, spa and barbecue area.

The Southwest

Abbey Beach Resort

595 Bussell Highway, Busselton; tel: 08-9755 4600; www.abbeybeach.com.au; $$$

Luxury beachside resort 7km (4.5 miles) from Busselton; one-, two- and three-bed apartments and studios with views over ocean or pool from the large balconies. Each has full kitchen, laundry and spa. Resort features include three pools, gym, squash, tennis, playground, bars and restaurant.

Blue Wren Travellers Rest YHA

17 Price Street, Denmark; tel: 08-9848 3300; www.denmarkbluewren.com.au; $

This town-centre backpackers hostel was purpose-built in 2001, with single, double and family rooms, as well as gender-specific dorms. The kitchen and laundry are bright, modern and well equipped. There's internet access and bicycles are available.

Busselton Jetty Chalets

94 Marine Terrace, Busselton; tel: 08-9752 3893; www.busseltonjettychalets.com; $$

Good value, comfortable, two-bed chalets are available here, with kitchens – no fuss and frills – positioned a short walk across a park to the beach and the famous jetty. Shared facilities include a barbecue area and playground.

Dunsborough Beach Cottages

95 Gifford Road, Dunsborough; tel: 08-9756 8885; www.dunsborough-beach.com.au; $$

With modern two- and three-bed, resort-style cottages on the white-sand beach of Geographe Bay, this place is only a short walk from shops and restaurants. Good facilities include a kitchen, log fires and outdoor area with barbecue, swimming pool and playground.

Dunsborough Central Motel

50 Dunn Bay Road, Dunsborough; tel: 08-9756 7711; www.dunsboroughmotel.com.au; $$

A town-centre motel in a garden setting with an outdoor pool, spa and barbecue area. One-bed spa rooms and two-bed superior rooms are on offer, all with kitchenette. Spa rooms have a dining area.

Dunsborough Inn

50 Dunn Bay Road, Dunsborough; tel: 08-9756 7277; www.dunsboroughinn.com; $

Reasonably modern budget accommodation attached to the Central Motel; offers self-contained units with en suite, through to non-dormitory hostel-style

rooms and backpacker facilities. There's a communal kitchen and dining room, with recreation areas.

Dunsborough Rail Carriages and Farm Cottages

123 Commonage Road, Dunsborough; tel: 08-9755 3865; www.dunsborough.com; $$$

Sleep in historic, beautifully presented, one-bed jarrah railway carriages at this stunning location, set in 40 hectares (100 acres) of farm and bushland 2km (1 mile) from town. All are en suite, with a veranda and a limited kitchen, and there's a shared barbecue. Two-bedroom cedar cottages are also available. Farm animals abound – as do kangaroos.

Forest Lodge Resort

Vasse Highway, Pemberton; tel: 08-9776 1113; www.forestlodgeresort.com.au; $$–$$$

An historic lodge among Karri forest, 2km (1 mile) from the town centre, with a range of accommodation: B&B guest rooms in the original lodge; two-bed chalets and studio motel units with a full kitchen, and the three-bed Homestead House, which suits large groups or families. The resort has extensive gardens, and a private lake where lessons in fly-fishing are given.

Karri Mia Bungalows

427 Mt Shadforth Road, Denmark; tel: 08-9848 2233; www.karrimia.com.au; $$$

Stunning accommodation overlooking the Karri forests, farmland, ocean views and vineyards of Denmark, in luxury spa, with self-contained two-bedroom chalets (some with spas) and one-bedroom studios.

Observatory Guest House

7 Brown Street, Busselton; tel: 08-9751 3336; www.observatoryguesthouse.com; $$$

A small, family owned B&B by Busselton Jetty, just 150 meters/yds from the sparkling shores of Geographe Bay. All four rooms are en suite. The tariff includes full breakfast, and there's a cute private garden with barbecue facilities.

Outback

Palace Hotel

137 Hannan Street, Kalgoorlie; tel: 08-9021 2788; www.palacehotelkalgoorlie.com; $$

A characterful hotel housed within an historic 19th-century stone building in the heart of the Goldfields. Herbert Hoover, who became US president in 1922, was a regular here when he was a 22-year-old mining engineer working in the Goldfields. A love letter he wrote to a barmaid is hung next to a mirror that he gifted the hotel before leaving.

Quality Inn Railway Motel

51 Forrest Street, Kalgoorlie; tel: 08-9088 0000; www.railwaymotel.com.au; $$

A central motel, facing the historic railway buildings, with rooms and self-contained units. Facilities include a pool and spa, and dinner and breakfast are served in Carriages restaurant.

The historic exterior of the Palace Hotel

North of Perth

Kalbarri Backpackers YHA
51 Mortimer Street, Kalbarri; tel: 08-9937 1430; www.kalbarribackpackers.com; $
A centrally located budget option with barbecue area, swimming pool, cooking facilities, laundry, food-and-drink, and bicycles for hire.

Kalbarri Palm Resort
8 Porter Street, Kalbarri; tel: 08-9937 2333; www.palmresort.com.au; $
Situated two minutes' walk from the harbour, beach, shops and restaurants, this is Kalbarri's earliest large-scale modern resort, with hotel-style rooms and two-bed family apartments with full cooking facilities. It has two swimming pools, tennis courts, bowls, cricket, a playground and barbecue area.

Ocean Centre Hotel
Foreshore Drive/Cathedral Avenue, Geraldton; tel: 08-9921 7777; www.oceancentrehotel.com.au; $$
This hotel benefits from being in the centre of town while also offering amazing ocean and harbour views. Modern well-appointed standard or deluxe rooms, some with private courtyard, others with balcony.

Ningaloo Reef and surrounds

Pelican Shore Villas
Grey Street/Kaiber Street, Kalbarri; tel: 08-9937 1708; www.pelicanshorevillas.com.au; $$$
This quality place offers very high-standard villas (sleeping up to 6 people), each with full kitchen and laundry. It's on the harbour road close to beaches and restaurants. The front villas overlook spectacular coastline and breaking surf.

RAC Monkey Mia Dolphin Resort
1 Monkey Mia Road, Monkey Mia, Shark Bay; tel: 08-9948 1320; www.parksandresorts.rac.com.au; $–$$$$
The only accommodation available in Monkey Mia (see page 97), this resort offers a range of options, from private rooms of various sizes (some complete with kitchenettes) to dorm rooms with shared bathrooms in a separate building with a communal kitchen.

Top End

Bali Hai Resort & Spa
6 Murray Road, Broome; tel: 08-9191 3100; www.balihairesort.com; $$$
Self-contained, Asian-influenced villas, reflecting Broome's multicultural character. Rooms offer courtyards and the novel luxury of showering under the stars in a private open air 'Mandi' bathroom.

Moonlight Bay Suites
51 Carnarvon Street, Broome; tel: 08-9195 5200; www.moonlightbaysuites.com.au; $$$
This hotel has a central situation in Broome, on the water's edge of Roebuck Bay. Half of the 50 suites overlook the water, so the Stairway to the Moon phenomenon can be seen from the property. Facilities include a great pool.

RESTAURANTS

Perth's potpourri population – which incorporates people from over 200 countries, many of them first-generation arrivals – is reflected in its fantastically diverse eating scene. A distinct Asian influence is very apparent throughout Western Australia, but cuisines and flavours from all over the planet can be found across the state, with innovative home-grown and imported chefs using excellent local ingredients, freshly harvested from the land and sea, and adding some cosmopolitan magic to make mouth-watering menus.

Central Perth

Annalakshmi

4 Barrack Square, Barrack Street Jetty; tel: 08-9221 3003; www.annalakshmi.com.au; daily noon–2pm, 6pm–9pm; $

You'll find fantastic vegetarian Indian fare here, on the banks of the Swan. Run by Hare Krishnas, the system at this ace restaurant is that you eat what you like and then pay what you think is fair. It has been operating like this for years and is justifiably very popular with locals and visitors.

Prices for two-course dinner for one, with a half-bottle of house wine:
$$$ = over A$40–60
$$ = A$40-60
$ = under A$40

Arirang Korean BBQ

91–93 Barrack Street; tel: 08-9225 4855; www.arirang.com.au; Mon–Fri 11.30am–3pm and 5pm–9.30pm, Sat–Sun 11.30am–9.30pm; $$

A popular traditional Korean barbecue restaurant, where hot coals are loaded under the barbecue plate at your table and you cook your choice of meat, creating little lettuce, rice, meat and sauce packages. Set menus come with miso soup, lettuce leaves, bean shoots, kimchi, sauces, rice and meat. Booking recommended on weekends. BYO booze.

Balthazar

6 The Esplanade, Elizabeth Quay; tel: 08-9421 1206; www.balthazar.com.au; Mon–Fri noon–3pm and 6pm–late, Sat 6pm–late; $$$

One for the discerning foodie, this dark, sophisticated restaurant serves some of the best food in Perth. Known for its massive and interesting wine list – the waiters are very knowledgeable and are happy to advise. Don't miss the potatoes fried in duck fat, but if you're feeling indecisive, try the ever-changing tasting plates (there's even a dessert-tasting plate). Best to book.

Belgian Beer Café

Westende, Cnr King and Murray Streets; tel: 08-9321 4094; www.belgianbeer.com.au; daily 11am–late; $$

A unique pub serving modern Belgian fare, including mussels, venison sausage and mouth-watering waffles. There is plenty of outdoor seating on the street or in the garden at the rear, where you can enjoy one of the beers on tap, including Hoegaarden, Leffe and Kriek. A cone of frites with aioli is a must.

Botanical Café

Fraser Avenue, Kings Park; tel: 08-9482 0122; www.botanicalcafe.com.au; daily 7am–7pm; $$

Location is everything here, and the Botanical boasts beautiful views across the park and Swan River. A casual restaurant with indoor and outdoor seating, it's open during daylight hours and does a cracking breakfast. Main meals can be accompanied by bottles of cleanskin West Australian wines, or handcrafted tap beers from the nearby Old Brewery.

C Restaurant Lounge

St Martin's Tower, level 33/44 St George's Terrace; tel: 08-9220 8333; www.crestaurant.com.au; daily 12.30–3.30pm and 6pm–late; $$$

On the 33rd storey of one of the city's office buildings, this revolving restaurant offers diners a 360-degree view of Perth, from Rottnest Island to Fremantle and across to the Perth Hills. The food is modern-Australian and elegant. Even if you don't want a full meal, reserve a table near the window in the bar and enjoy a couple of first-rate cocktails while watching the sun set.

Fraser's Restaurant

Fraser Avenue, Kings Park; tel: 08-9481 7100; www.frasersrestaurant.com.au; daily noon–late; $$$

An iconic Perth venue with killer views, where executive chef Chris Taylor uses top-quality Western Australian produce in a varied menu with dishes ranging from roast kangaroo loin with potato and celeriac crumble, beetroot and caramelised onion, to chargrilled WA rock lobster with spicy tomato sauce.

Matilda Bay Restaurant

3 Hackett Drive, Crawley, Matilda Bay; tel: 08-9423 5000; www.matildabayrestaurant.com.au; Mon–Sat 11am–late, Sun 11am–3pm; $$$

Situated on the banks of the Swan River at Matilda Bay, this restaurant is popular for its beautiful views and peaceful location, making it a good option for a special occasion at reasonable cost. Try the grilled barramundi fillet, mango cream purée and lime coconut crusted scallops.

Nine Mary's

Corner Hay and Milligan streets; tel: 08-9226 4999; www.9marys.com; Mon–Fri 11.30am–2.30pm and 5.30–9.30pm, Sat 5.30–9.30pm; $$

A light and bright restaurant serving traditional Indian cuisine. An extensive menu includes good tandoori, alongside a range of curries, from mild butter chicken to the fragrant (lamb saag) and the hot (pork vindaloo). Try the mixed tasting plate for starters.

Taka's Kitchen

150–152 Barrack Street; tel: 08-9324 1234;
www.takaskitchen.iinet.net.au; Mon–Sat
11am–9pm, Sun 11am–5.30pm; $

The emphasis is on speed and value at
this frenetic Japanese café, which serves
a range of dishes (including agedashi
tofu, chicken katsu, teriyaki fish and
sashimi). All meals are available in small
or large. There is free tea and a range of
help-yourself sauces. The quality is reasonable, especially at such low prices.

Zafferano

173 Mounts Bay Road, Crawley; tel: 08-
9321 2588; www.zafferano.com.au; daily
11am–late; $$$$

Situated in the historic Swan Brewery complex, this high-end restaurant
boasts some of the prettiest views of
the city at night. The menu offers classic
Italian seafood dishes, including melt-in-
your-mouth crayfish, seafood risotto and
their famous creamy seafood chowder.
The atmosphere and service are upmarket, so it's perfect for a special dinner.
When booking ask for a table with a view.

East Perth and south of the Swan

The Boatshed

Coode Street Jetty, Coode Street; tel: 08-
9474 1314; www.boatshedrestaurant.com;
Mon–Sat 8am till late, Sun 8–4pm; $$$

A south-side water-view favourite
for all times of the day, thanks to the
180-degree views of the Swan River,
Perth City and Kings Park, available

from the café and the restaurant. Serves
modern, locally sourced fare (including
WA nettle pesto, and WA swimmer crab
risotto) and invites you to BYO.

Ciao Italia

273 Mill Point Road, South Perth; tel: 08-
9368 5500; www.ciaoitalia.com.au; Tue–Sat
5–10pm; $$

This small, authentic eatery radiates
traditional Italian cuisine and atmosphere that keeps people coming back.
There is a huge amount to choose from
on the menu and the pizzas are particularly good, with thin crispy bases. The
restaurant does not take bookings and
is packed out every night of the week so
get in early. BYO welcome.

Mends Street Café

Shop 2/35 Mends Street, South Perth;
tel: 08-9367 7332; daily 7am–10pm; $$

A waterside favourite offering great food at
any time of the day, this is a relaxed spot
to chill out with a coffee and a cake while
reading the newspapers, or to tuck into a
burger after a walk along the riverbank.

Viet Royal

Corner Royal and Plain streets; tel: 08-9221
2388; www.vietroyalperth.com; Tue–Fri
11.30am–2pm & 5pm–late, Sat–Mon 5pm–
late; $$

Traditional Vietnamese cuisine showcasing the best this style of cooking has
to offer. The atmosphere is calm and
comfortable, reflecting owner Kim Ha's
gentle and generous personality. You

Fraser's Restaurant offers fantastic views

can also BYO, and, conveniently, there's a bottle shop just a short stroll away.

Subiaco and Leederville

Boucla

349 Rokeby Road, Subiaco; tel: 08-9381 2841; www.boucla.com.au; Mon–Sat 7am–4pm, Sun 8am–1pm; $

Boucla is a Byzantine treat. Fight your way past Turkish rugs and Greek statues to the counter where there are no menus and no price lists. All food is cooked fresh that day, and whatever is on display is what's left. There are often spanakopitas, roast veg salads, koto-pita and lamb pies, plus lots of Greek shortbreads and cakes.

Cheers Japanese Restaurant

375 Hay Street; tel: 08-9388 2044; daily noon–2.30pm and 6–9pm; $

This authentic Japanese restaurant is somewhat hidden behind a group of shops on Hay Street. If you're with a group, make sure you ask for one of the traditional tables where you take off your shoes and let your feet dangle into the well under the table. Order a range of dishes to share.

Delizioso

94 Rokeby Road; tel: 08-9381 7796; www. delisio.com.au; Mon–Tue 4–9pm, Wed–Sat 8am–9pm, Sun 5–9pm; $

The best thing about this little café is its Italian pizza, served by the slice. Tasty toppings include eggplant and chilli, potato and rosemary and straight cheese and herbs.

Duende

662 Newcastle Street, Leederville; tel: 08-9228 0123; www.duende.com.au; daily noon–late; $$$

A little slice of Europe, serving fabulous tapas, cheese and other tasty tidbits in an elegant yet funky setting. Ask for some help with the wine list and perhaps even let the waiter choose one for you. It is the sort of place to enjoy a long leisurely evening with lots of tapas and divine wine, and good conversation with friends.

Funtastico

12 Rokeby Road; tel: 08-9381 2688; www. funtastico.com.au; Tue–Thu and Sat–Sun noon–3pm and 5pm–9pm, Fri noon–9pm; $$

If you could get upmarket casual, this would be it. Favoured by folk about town for its good pastas and sensational pizzas, it has great alfresco seating.

Lanna Thai Cuisine

375 Hay Street, Subiaco; tel: 08-9381 2766; www.lannathai.com.au; daily 5pm–late; $$

The extensive menu features soups, entrées, lots of vegetarian options, dry and wet curries, noodle dishes and desserts. The lovely things about Thai cuisine – fresh herbs, chilli, lime, light ingredients – are all evident in owner Kitty's food. The ambience is good too, with a warm Thai welcome.

Ria

106 Oxford Street, Leederville; tel: 08-9328 2998; www.riamalaykitchen.com.au; daily 5–10pm; $$$

With a menu reflecting Malaysia's melting pot of cultures and cuisines, dishes here are a fantastic fusion of flavours from Malaysia, India, China and Portugal (the vindaloo recipe is an Iberian one). Meals aren't cheap, but the food is amazing. Be sure to book.

The Subiaco Hotel

Corner Hay Street and Rokeby Road; tel: 08-9381 3069; www.subiacohotel.com.au; Mon–Fri 7am–midnight, Sat–Sun 8am–midnight; $$

'The Subi' is a popular pub-restaurant with a sports bar, a more upmarket cocktail bar and a restaurant, which has outdoor veranda seating on Hay Street, indoor seating and a rear garden. The inventive, inspired food ranges from Shark Bay crab linguini and Linely Valley pork belly to vegetarian options like house-made gnocchi, hazelnut cream, wild mushrooms, goat's cheese and chestnuts. Booking is advisable.

Northbridge

The Brass Monkey

209 William Street, corner of James Street, Northbridge; tel: 08-9227 9596; www.thebrassmonkey.com.au; Sun–Tue 10am–midnight, Wed–Thu 10am–1pm, Fri–Sat 10am–2am; $$

If you fancy a bite with your beer, the Brass Menu in this long-established Northbridge watering hole includes traditional pub grub – hotdogs, wings, ribs and pizzas – and you can place and scoff your order from any bar in the venue. The kitchen remains open all the time the pub is serving.

The Brisbane Hotel

292 Beaufort Street, Highgate; tel: 08-9227 2300; www.thebrisbanehotel.com.au; Mon–Sat 11.30am–10pm, Sun 11.30am–9pm; $$

Possibly the most stylish hotel in Perth, the Brisbane is relaxed and funky. You can pop in for a drink, but the food is worth staying for, so grab a table in the shady garden. The pizzas are excellent, as are the more substantial mains, such as grilled fish on Asian greens and prawn fettucine.

The Flying Scotsman

639 Beaufort Street, Mt Lawley; tel: 08-9328 6200; www.theflyingscotto.com; daily 11am till late; $$

An English-style pub serving top-notch pub grub, including burgers and pizzas, with pleasingly generous portions.

Nine Fine Food

227–9 Bulwer Street, Highgate; tel: 08-9227 9999; www.ninefinefood.com.au; Tue–Thu 6pm–10pm, Fri–Sat 6pm–10.30pm; $$$

Chef-owner Muneki Song creates elegant, modern Japanese cuisine here (duck ramen, tempura vegetables and seafood, miso ribs), with a hint of European influence thrown in. The restaurant has a nice ambience. Try the excellent degustation menu, and BYO wine.

Tarts Café

212 Lake Street, Northbridge; tel: 08-9328 6607; www.tartscafe.com.au; daily

Kailis Fish Market Café

7am–5pm, also Wed–Fri 5.30–10pm; $
A lovely spot nestled among the terrace homes on Lake Street. For breakfast try the scrambled eggs with feta, wilted spinach, oven-roasted tomatoes and rosemary flavoured Turkish bread. Great coffees too. Look out for special Friday night degustation events (Scandinavian, Bavarian, Italian)

Fremantle

Benny's Bar and Café
10–12 South Terrace; tel: 08-9433 1333; www.bennys.com.au; Mon–Thu 7.30am–midnight, Fri 7.30am–1am, Sat from 8am–1am, Sun 8am–midnight; $$
An all-day food and music institution, serving café-style dishes and fusion food, as well as filling Italian cuisine. Pop in for oysters, cocktails and live jazz or settle in for some Freo people-watching on the Cappuccino Strip.

Capri Restaurant
21 South Terrace; tel: 08-9335 1399; www.caprirestaurantfremantle.com; Tue–Sun noon–2pm and 5–9.30pm, Mon 5–9.30pm, $
The Capri has been a part of the Fremantle eating scene for over 20 years. It still gives diners a complimentary bowl of minestrone soup and bread on arrival. The atmosphere is homely and the food basic but tasty.

Char Char Bull
44b Mews Road, Fishing Boat Harbour; tel: 08-9335 7666; www.charcharrb.com.

au; Mon–Thu 11.30am–3pm, 5.30pm–late, Fri–Sun 11.30am–late; $$$
Offering a classic surf-and-turf experience in a great location, the large menu here encompasses prime beef, kangaroo, seafood and pizza. There's also a popular cocktail bar for pre-dinner drinks.

Kailis Fish Market Café
46 Mews Road, Fishing Boat Harbour; tel: 08-9335 7755; www.kailis.com/fremantle; daily 10am–8pm; $
Kailis has been providing Perth and Fremantle with seafood for over 75 years. Tourists and locals flock to its waterside location. The fresh seafood market resides at one end of the large store, and the café functions at the other, with ample seating outside on the jetty. There's basic fish and chips, plus a variety of salads, grills and desserts.

Little Creatures
10 Mews Road; tel: 08-9430 5555; www.littlecreatures.com.au; daily 10am–late, Sat–Sun from 9am; $$
Once a crocodile farm, this huge shed now houses one of WA's best breweries. Serving its own beer and a range of wine, its semi-industrial yet welcoming interior draws huge crowds. The food is good, too – try the frites with aioli, the mussels or any of the pizzas.

Old Shanghai at Fremantle Markets
4 Henderson Street; tel: 08-9336 7676;

Wed–Sun 10am–9pm; www.oldshanghai.
com.au; $
This food hall has a range of great-value
Asian cuisines. Taka's Kitchen is budget
Japanese, Ray's Curry House produces
a fantastic fish curry served with roti,
and there are vendors selling Thai,
Malay, Indo and Chinese food. You can
also buy alcohol and freshly squeezed
juices.

Sala Thai
22 Norfolk Street; tel: 08-9335 7749; www.
salathai.com.au; daily 6pm–9pm, Fri–Sat
until 9.30pm; $$
Unpretentious, quality Thai cuisine
with a menu featuring all the favourites
(Pad Thai, green and red curry, stuffed
chicken wings, duck dishes) in a relaxed
setting. The staff are warm and the food
has a lovely fresh zing, so typical of Thai.
Good-quality ingredients and attentive
service.

Beaches

The Blue Duck
151 Marine Parade, Cottesloe; tel: 08-
9385 2499; www.blueduck.com.au; daily
6.30am–9pm; $$
This eatery overlooking the ocean at
North Cottesloe is an institution. For
early birds, à la carte breakfasts start at
7am. From lunchtime it's always busy,
and you'll have to book to get a table
with a sea view. The menu focuses on
seafood, but you'll find many other
options, from sticky sweet-and-sour
pork to saffron risotto, mustard lamb

rack and pizzas. If nothing else, come
for coffee and scrambled eggs while
enjoying the early morning light.

Voyage Kitchen
128a West Coast Drive, Sorrento; tel: 08-
9447 2443; www.voyagesorrento.com.au;
daily 6am–late; $$
This is a great little establishment serv-
ing interesting food, such as Moroc-
can chicken with couscous and elegant
open steak sandwiches. You can also
buy takeaway salads and lovely bottled
oils and jams. The coffee is strong, the
interior light and bright and the staff
provide a warm welcome.

Swan Valley

The Guildford Hotel
159 James Street, Guildford; tel: 08-9460
9966; www.theguildfordhotel.com.au; daily
11am–late; $$
Like a phoenix, this old pub has risen
from the flames of a devastating fire to
reclaim its reputation as an amazing
heritage building and a fine pub with
an outstanding menu. If you're hungry,
try the Pitmaster: a selection of slow-
cooked smoked meats (pork beef lamb
and chicken) with sides. A feast for at
least four people, for $120.

Darlington Estate
39 Nelson Road, Darlington; tel: 08-9299
6268; www.darlingtonestate.com.au; Thu–
Sun lunch, Fri–Sat dinner; $$$
The food at this winery restaurant is
sublime. The style is European, with

The Little Creatures Brewery restaurant serves good food and even better beer

well-balanced flavours. The signature dish is a lamb shank wrapped in pastry, but try the rare kangaroo loin for something different. The wines are good and the views are beautiful.

Duckstein Brewery

9720 West Swan Road, Henley Brook; tel: 08-9296 0620; www.duckstein.com.au; Sun–Thu 11am–5pm, Fri–Sat 11am–late; $$

This German brewery not only makes excellent beer, but has a huge list of German food to accompany it. The Brewer's Pan – a fry packed with pan-fried potatoes, kassler smoked pork cutlets and bratwurst sausages – is recommended.

North of Perth

La Perle Restaurant

10 Murray Street, within Kimberley Sands Resort and Spa, Cable Beach, Broome; tel: 08-9193 8300; daily 7am–9pm; $$$

Offering elegant French cuisine, using standout local Western Australian produce, the sophisticated menu here (from the seared scallops to the creme brûlée with berries and macadamia shortbread) matches the amazing setting, between native bushland and a luxury pool.

Restaurant Upstairs

Porter Street, Kalbarri; www.upstairsrestaurant.com.au; tel: 08-9937 1033; Thu–Mon 4pm–10pm, Fri–Sun outside school holidays; $

Both the food and ambience are great here, with a beautiful view of the river mouth and ocean. The interior is fresh and modern, with changing artworks from all around Australia.

Skeeta's Restaurant and Café

101 Foreshore Drive, Geraldton; tel: 08-9964 1619; www.skeetas.com.au; daily 6.30am–11pm; $$

Skeeta's specialises in seafood, yet they've got the non-fish eaters covered, too, with pasta, steak and chicken dishes. The whiting fillets served with crispy gourmet potatoes and salad are a favourite, as is the seafood platter for two.

South of Perth

Aristos Waterfront

15 Bonnefoi Boulevard, Bunbury; tel: 08-9791 6477; www.aristosbunbury.com.au; 11am–late; $$

Stunningly situated over the water at the Marlston Hill development, Aristos serves fresh seafood along with regular fish and chips. Coffee, cakes and wine are available as well.

Equinox Café

343 Queen Street, Busselton; tel: 08-9752 4641; www.theequinox.com.au; daily 8am–late; $$

This waterfront restaurant is surrounded by lovely Moreton Bay fig trees and has a beautiful view of the ocean. Its interesting Australian and international cuisine is as popular with locals as it is with tourists.

Mojos is full of personality

NIGHTLIFE

In terms of dusk-til-dawn shenanigans, the west coast of Australia has a completely different feel to the east coast, which focuses heavily on the boozy backpacker party circuit, with themed nightclubs and barn-sized pubs featuring live entertainment aimed at a very young, predominantly British and Irish crowd. Of course there are plenty of after-dark drinking dens offering cheap deals to budget-conscious backpackers here too – and in the mineral-rich areas of the outback, where miners like to rinse the red dust from their pores with a few beers, it can get pretty raucous. But this definitely isn't the backbone of the evening scene in the cities.

The west traditionally attracts slightly more mature travellers, many wooed by WA's wine trails and reputation for boutique breweries, who mingle well with local nighthawks in surprisingly sophisticated bars and clubs in Perth and Fremantle, where there are also many LGBTQ-friendly venues. Northbridge is the epicentre of club culture, and the place where the bold, the beautiful and the best-dressed Perthites go to sip expensive cocktails and wrap their ears around the latest tunes.

There is a very healthy live music scene in Western Australia, which cuts across all genres. Various venues support local, national and international acts. Keep your eye on billboards and

the street press, and you may find yourself watching bands with global followings – like Pendulum or Tame Impala – in front of a home crowd, or a group that's considered 'big' in Britain or the US in an intimate pub or club setting in Perth or Fremantle.

For those with higher brows, Perth is the best bet for a decent dose of evening drama. The Cultural Centre, in between the city centre and Northbridge, is the major hub of the city's theatrical output. The following is just a very small selection of what else is on offer.

Perth

The Bird
181 William Street; www.williamstreetbird.com
With a signature sound that's a lot more indie, this chilled venue stages performances from alternative local and visiting bands, plus DJs, in its main bar and also under the stars in the outdoor courtyard area.

Connections
81 James Street, Northbridge; www.connectionsnightclub.com
With a wild history going back 45 years, Perth's premier gay and lesbian nightclub has been a hotspot for the LGBTQ community since 1975, and the party continues apace. A cracking DJ line-up, unpretentious dance floor, drag queen performers and amazing

outdoor terrace attracts people of all persuasions.

Geisha Bar

135a James Street, Northbridge; www.geishabar.com.au

An intimate, small venue, which bigs itself up as Perth's most decadent nightclub, an upmarket sonic temple of underground sounds, designer teez and colourful cocktails, where local fashion arbiters and rising stars rub shoulders with interstate visitors and jet-setting internationals.

Metro City

146 Roe Street; www.metroconcertclub.com

A mid- to large-sized entertainment hub featuring club nights and hosting international DJs, bands and theatrical performances across an eclectic range of genres.

Mint

139 James Street, Northbridge; www.mintnightclub.com

A retro-themed (and retro dec'd) place playing the best of the 80s, 90s and 00s during Club Retro Friday, and party anthems during Pop Life Saturday. No cover charge to early arrivers (pre 9pm). Licensed until 5am.

Rocket Room

174 James Street, Northbridge; www.rocketroom.com.au

A Tardis-like venue that doesn't promise much from the outside, the Rocket Room Radical Review Bar is one of city's most rocking live music venues, with bands pumping out the power chords four nights a week (Wednesday to Saturday).

Fremantle

The Metropolis

58 South Terrace, Fremantle; www.metropolisfremantle.com.au

This large, somewhat impersonal performance space has been welcoming international acts and big local bands and DJs for decades. Drinks are pricey, so perhaps explore the excellent Sail and Anchor Hotel next door first.

Mojos

237 Queen Victoria Street, North Fremantle; www.mojosbar.com.au

With much more personality than the bigger venues, Mojos makes the most of its modest (but very cool) surrounds to showcase original live music, alternative sounds and comedy all week, 'local and foreign, hard and soft, new and old, obvious and obscure, friendly and furious'.

Bunbury

Vat 2

2 Jetty Road, Bunbury; www.vat2.com.au

Hosting live bands on the beach (including the likes of local high-fliers Birds of Tokyo), this venue is a popular drinking spot and eating joint, aa well as hosting JB's Beach Club, where drinks are served on the sand.

A–Z

A

Admission charges

Compared with the UK and USA, admission charges to sights and attractions are fairly low, and museums are often free. The Museum and the Art Gallery of WA, for example, are free except for special exhibitions. Concession rates are available in many places on production of a senior or student card.

Age restrictions

By law, to drink alcohol, smoke tobacco or get a tattoo in Western Australia you must be 18 or over. Drivers in WA must be 17 years of age to obtain a licence; visitors under 18 years of age will not be able to hire rental cars, and those under 25 will pay a premium.

B

Budgeting

During the recent mining boom, WA was awash with money and prices for everything from pints and pies to accommodation became a little alarming for visitors. It's still not a cheap place to travel around, but things have settled a little bit, and there is plenty to enjoy for nothing.

Accommodation. A bed at a back-packer hostel can be as little as A$25 a night, and a room in a three-star hotel is usually around A$100. A room in a four- or five-star hotel can start as low as A$200. Internet and low-season deals can halve advertised tariffs.

Airport taxi. A taxi from Perth Airport to central Perth will cost around A$50.

Car rental. Renting a small car costs from A$125 per week; a 4WD will cost around A$200 per week. Petrol (gasoline) costs around A$1.20 per litre (more expensive in the outback).

Restaurants. A main course in a budget restaurant costs about A$15, A$20–30 at a moderate restaurant, and A$30–50 at an expensive restaurant. A bottle of Australian wine from a bottle shop (liquor store) starts at about A$8; the same bottle in a restaurant is likely to cost A$18, hence the popularity of BYO (Bring Your Own) restaurants. A glass of house wine averages around A$8. A pint of full-strength draught beer frequently costs around A$10, although pressure has forced prices down as low as A$3 recently, and a cup of coffee is around A$3.50.

C

Children

Australia is a great place to travel with kids, and WA is particularly well suited to young families, with wide, wild open spaces, lots of parks and playgrounds, and loads of animal encounters, from meeting kangaroos on Heirisson Island and quokkas on

Cooling off in a fountain

Rottnest, to feeding dolphins in Monkey Mia and snorkelling on accessible areas of Ningaloo reef. Indigenous experiences can be transformative. Almost all museums and attractions allow little ones in for nothing (child-concession admission usually applies to children 12 years and under, but it can be as old as 16).

Climate

Perth's Mediterranean-style climate has four distinctive seasons, although the sun shines most days. Rainfall has decreased alarmingly in recent years, but the long-term pattern is for most of the year's rain to fall during the winter months, June–August, easing off in spring. The city is often dry for months on end, and summer can be very hot, with temperatures rising well above 35°C (95°F). Average temperatures are: winter 18°C (65°F), spring (September–November) 22°C (72°F), summer (December–February) 32°C (86°F), autumn (March–May) 24°C (75°F). These temperatures sound high, but WA's low humidity makes them bearable, and the reliable breeze known as the Fremantle Doctor, which rolls in off the Indian Ocean, is a relief.

Clothing

In most scenarios across WA, dress is informal and casual, though some hotels, restaurants and clubs will require a jacket and tie in the evening. Lightweight clothing is suitable year-round, but bring a jumper and waterproof coat for evenings and trips to the southwest, especially in autumn and winter. In the tropical north, dress is always informal, with very few restaurants and clubs requiring a jacket and tie. Lightweight clothing is suitable all year round. To protect yourself against sunstroke and sunburn, you should wear sunscreen, a broad-brimmed hat, good sunglasses and a shirt with collar and sleeves. Bring swimwear and rash vests (tight fitting, quick drying tops) for the beach.

Crime and safety

Perth, Fremantle and most of WA are generally fairly safe, but do not leave valuables unattended or in parked cars. Avoid dark, empty spaces and public toilets at night, and be aware of the potential for alcohol-fuelled violence around nightclubs. The police are helpful and competent.

Customs

Non-dutiable allowances are 25g (0.9oz) of tobacco goods (25 cigarettes) and 2.25 litres of beer, wine or spirits, and other dutiable goods to the total value of A$900, plus personal clothing, footwear and toiletries. Up to A$450-worth of dutiable goods, not including alcohol or tobacco, are allowed in the baggage of children under 18. Visit www.homeaffairs.gov.au for further information.

Strict quarantine regulations forbid the importation of foods, plants, animals and their by-products. Heavy jail penalties apply to the smuggling of drugs of any kind. Visitors are allowed to carry up to four weeks' supply of

Forest fire

prescribed medications, but for larger supplies you should carry a doctor's certificate for customs purposes.

D

Disabled travellers

Generally speaking, awareness about disability in WA is good, with rights of access enshrined in law. A website detailing WA's major disability service providers, **People with Disabilities WA** (www.pwdwa.org) is very useful. **Tourism WA** (www.westernaustralia.com) details accessible accommodation, restaurants and tours, and the **National Public Toilet Map** (www.toiletmap.gov.au) lists thousands of public toilets around Australia, including those with wheelchair access in WA.

Driving

Drive on the left at all times in Australia. When driving in the outback always carry lots of water, check your spare tyre/jack/oil, fill up with fuel at every opportunity and, if you do breakdown, stay with your vehicle. Give road trains plenty of space on the road.

E

Electricity

Electrical power is 240/250v AC, 50Hz Universal. Most hotels also have outlets for 110v (shavers only). Adaptors for Australian power outlets are readily available at the airport and in shops and hotels.

Embassies and consulates

The following are the closest contacts for travellers needing assistance when in WA.

British Consular Agency, Level 12/251 Adelaide Terrace, Perth WA 6000; tel: 08-9224 4700

Canadian Consulate General, 267, St George's Terrace, 3rd Floor, Perth, WA 6000; tel: 08-9322 7930

Consulate General of Ireland, 1/100 Terrace Road, East Perth, WA 6004; tel: 08-6557 5802

US Consulate General, Level 4/16 St Georges Terrace, Perth WA 6000; tel: 08-6144 5100

Emergencies

In an emergency, dial 000 for police, fire or ambulance services. From a mobile (cell phone), also try dialling 112. For police attendance in non-life-threatening situations dial 131 444.

H

Health

Australia has excellent medical services. For medical attention out of working hours go to the casualty department of a major hospital or, if the matter is less urgent, visit one of the medical clinics in the major towns and tourist centres. Look under 'medical centres' or 'medical practitioners' online, or ask at your hotel.

Sun protection is essential

Pride Parade, Northbridge

Healthcare and insurance

Citizens of countries with which Australia has a reciprocal agreement (UK, Ireland, Finland, Norway, Sweden, Malta, Netherlands, New Zealand) are allowed restricted access to government Medicare service; this covers free care as a patient in hospital and subsidised medicines. It does not cover dental care, ambulance costs or emergency evacuation to your home country, so you are advised to take out your own travel insurance. Visitors from other countries should have private insurance to cover all medical care. See www.health.gov.au for details.

Inoculations

No vaccinations are necessary for entry into Australia unless you have visited an area (including parts of South America and Africa) infected by yellow fever, cholera or typhoid in the previous 14 days.

Natural Health Hazards

The biggest danger for travellers in Australia is the sun. Even on mild, cloudy days it has the potential to burn. Wear a broad-brimmed hat and, if you are planning on being out for a while, a long-sleeved shirt made from a light fabric. Wear SPF 30+ sunblock at all times, even under a hat.

Apart from stingers (jellyfish which can deliver a painful sting, prevalent November–March in coastal water north of Geraldton), the main danger in north WA's s tropical waters are saltwater (or estuarine) crocodiles. Do not enter water where crocodile warning signs are posted, always ask for local advice, and if in doubt do not venture in. Some species of shark do pose a potential risk, albeit not as big as most people's fears lead them to believe. To be extra cautious, avoid swimming in murky water, with dogs or close to where pipes pump water or waste out to sea.

Pharmacies and hospitals

'Chemist shops' are a great place to go for advice on minor ailments such as bites, scratches and stomach trouble. They also stock a wide range of useful products such as sunblock, nappies (diapers) and non-prescription drugs. If you have a prescription from your doctor, and you want to take it to a pharmacist in Australia, you will need to have it endorsed by a local medical practitioner.

L

LGBTQ travellers

Western Australia may not have quite the same gay sub-culture that you would find in Sydney, but there is a thriving gay community in Perth. The age of consent is 16, the same as for heterosexuals. Several entertainment and accommodation establishments cater for the gay scene, and in the club and nightlife sectors many more are totally accepting of gay and lesbian people. **Living Proud LGBTI Community Services of WA** (formerly Gay & Lesbian Community Services of WA; tel: 08-9486 9855; www.living-proud.org.au) is a non-profit organisation

which aims to promote the wellbeing of lesbian, gay, bisexual, trans, intersex, queer and other sexuality, sex and gender diverse people in Western Australia.

Lost property

Report loss or theft of valuables to the police immediately, as most insurance policies insist on a police report.

In Australia the federal government recently changed the laws relating to compensation for lost air luggage, and travellers will now be covered by the Montreal Convention, allowing for fairer compensation on lost items and removing compensation caps.

M

Media

TV and radio

The ABC (Australian Broadcasting Corporation; www.abc.net.au) and Special Broadcasting Service (SBS; www.sbs.com.au) are best for up-to-the-minute news. National broadcast TV is Channel 2; national radio, FM 97.7, and AM 810 and AM 585; local radio AM 720. Triple J (99.3 FM in Perth, or listen online from anywhere www.abc.net.au/triplej) offers rock and comment for the twentysomethings; tourist information radio is on FM 87.6. Most commercial radio stations are music-oriented, punctuated by brief news bulletins and less-brief advertising segments.

SBS national TV carries various foreign-language news programmes in the morning and good world news coverage every evening at 6.30pm. Local community Channel 44 shows Aljazeera and is also strong on local events, tourist information, restaurant reviews, etc. Commercial TV stations are channels 7, 9 and 10, and they carry most of the high-profile sports events.

Foxtel (www.foxtel.com.au) is the major pay television company in the country, operating cable, direct broadcast satellite television and IPTV services. Many hotels provide access to a large number of cable television stations.

Print and online media

The *West Australian* (www.thewest.com.au) is Perth's only daily newspaper (Monday–Saturday), and the *Sunday Times* (www.perthnow.com.au) is the only Sunday paper. Australia has two national papers, the *Australian* (www.theaustralian.com.au) and the *Australian Financial Review* (www.afr.com). Foreign-language newspapers and magazines are available at newsagents in Perth, the airport and major tourist districts.

The Australian is a national paper, printed in Perth and available Monday–Saturday. Weekly news magazines include the *Bulletin* and *Time*. English-language weekly compilations from UK newspapers – *Telegraph*, *Express*, *Guardian* – are available at most newsagents.

Online

Australia's media is more or less dominated by two powerful groups, News Ltd and Packer's PBL. Alternative views

Currency exchange facilities can be found in major towns and cities

flourish only on the internet; www. crikey.com.au is one of the best for its take – generally scathing, often humorous – on politics, business, sport and other matters Australian. The Conversation (www.theconversation.com/au) is an independent, not-for-profit online media outlet with good in-depth articles about various issues, and the *Guardian Australia*, a dedicated Australia-focussed incarnation of the global online publication and British print newspaper, *The Guardian*, is also available online (www.theguardian.com/au).

Money

The four major banks in Australia are ANZ, Commonwealth, National Australia and Westpac. There's also Perth-based Bankwest, previously known as The Bank of Western Australia (www. bankwest.com.au). Trading hours are generally Mon–Thu 9am–4pm and Fri 9am–5pm.

Cash machines

Most bank branches have automatic teller machines (ATMs) that are networked with Cirrus, Maestro and other networks, allowing you to access funds from overseas accounts. Many will charge you to withdraw cash.

Credit cards

Most establishments display a list of the credit cards they will accept, usually including MasterCard and Visa, and less so Amex, Diners Club and JCB.

Currency

Australia's currency is the dollar (A$), which is divided into 100 cents. Notes come in denominations of 5, 10, 20, 50 and 100 dollars, each of which has a distinctly different colour. Coins come in denominations of 5, 10, 20 and 50 cents (silver-coloured), and one and two dollars (bronze-coloured). The one-dollar coin is, confusingly, larger than the two. There are no one- or two-cent coins, so shopkeepers round change to the nearest five cents.

Taxes

The Australian government collects a 10 percent goods and services tax (GST) on virtually all retail sales. Under a 'tourist refund scheme', the GST on goods valued at over A$300, bought from the same shop within the previous 30 days and carried as hand luggage, can be recovered upon leaving the country at a Tourist Refund Scheme (TRS) booth located beyond customs at the airport; you must have retained the tax invoice. For more details (www.customs.gov.au/site/page4646.asp).

Tipping

Tipping is not customary even for taxi drivers and restaurant staff, but it is not unusual to reward good service with a gratuity of between 10 and 15 percent of the bill. Hotel staff do not solicit or expect tips, but certainly will not be offended by one.

Australian Post office

O

Opening hours

Core business hours are Mon–Thu 9am–5.30pm, Fri until 9pm in the cities, Sat 9am–1pm. However, retailers tend to follow demand, and hours vary widely, with most shops in tourist precincts open on Saturday afternoon and Sunday.

P

Post

Australian Post (www.auspost.com.au) offices are open Mon–Fri 9am–5pm; some post shops are also open Sat 9am–noon. Post offices will hold properly addressed mail for visitors and sell stamps, standard and Express Post envelopes and packaging. Post boxes are red (standard mail) or yellow (Express Post).

The cost of overseas mail depends on the weight and size of the package. To send a postcard to Europe or the USA costs A$2.60. A letter up to 50g in weight will also cost A$2.60.

Public holidays

Banks, post offices, government and private offices close on the following holidays:
New Year's Day (1 Jan)
Australia Day (26 Jan)
Labour Day (first Monday in March)
Good Friday (date variable)
Easter Monday (date variable)
Anzac Day (25 April)
Western Australia Day (First Monday in June)
Queen's Birthday (last Monday in September)
Christmas Day (25 Dec)
Boxing Day (26 Dec)

T

Telephones

Although they're becoming rarer, there are still over 24,000 working payphones across Australia. Local calls from public phones cost 50 cents. Long-distance calls to Australian and overseas numbers can be made from most phones. Some public phones operate by card, available from post offices, large newsagents, etc. For up-to-date rates and information, make a toll-free call to Telstra on 1800 011 433.

Overseas calls

The exit code from Australia is 0011, followed by the country code and number, for example France (33); Germany (49); Indonesia (62); Italy (39); Japan (81); Netherlands (31); Philippines (63); Spain (34); UK (44); USA and Canada (1).

Mobile (cell) phones

The GSM 900 mobile phone system network in Australia is compatible with systems everywhere except Japan and the Americas. To use your mobile here for a short term you should buy an Australian SIM card with prepaid calls. Providers include Telstra (www.telstra.

Public telephone   *Airport check-in facility*

com), Optus (www.optus.com.au), Vodaphone (www.vodafone.com.au) and Virgin Mobile (www.virginmobile.com.au).

Time zones

All of Western Australia, including Perth, is eight hours in advance of Greenwich Mean Time. Australia's eastern states are 1.5 or 2 hours ahead of Perth. Because they operate a daylight-saving system, and WA does not, the eastern states are 2.5–3 hours ahead between October and March.

Toilets

Department stores, Wellington Street railway station, museums and other public buildings and places all have toilet facilities. In addition, automatic toilet booths are situated at the west end of James Street, in Northbridge, and in the Cultural Centre. You will also find toilets in the changing rooms of the larger beaches.

Tourist information

Before you leave home, see the Tourism Australia website, www.australia.com. Western Australia is well served by organisations designed to help visitors. In addition to information centres, the following website will answer almost any questions that you might have (www.westernaustralia.com).

Transport

Airports

Many international airlines provide regular links between Perth Airport (www.perthairport.com.au) and Europe, the US and Asian and Pacific nations. Frequent Qantas, Virgin and Rex domestic services fly to and from Perth from Sydney, Melbourne, Canberra and other state capitals, as well as regional destinations such as Monkey Mia, Broome and Albany. **Perth Airport** is served by buses and taxis. Few hotels provide regular courtesy coach transfers, but some will do so on request. Cabs to the city are expensive (around $50).

Public transport

Transwa (www.transwa.wa.gov.au) is responsible for public transport by bus, train and ferry throughout the region. The Perth Central Area Transit bus (Perth CAT), which serves central areas in Perth city, Fremantle and Joondalup, is free. There's also a SmartRider Free Transit Zone for trains

Rail and long-distance bus

Perth Railway Station is the largest station on the Transperth network (www.transperth.wa.gov.au). Trains from here service the Armadale, Fremantle, Joondalup, Mandurah and Midland lines as well as Transwa's Australind service to Bunbury. **Transwa** operate three passenger train services to locations across WA: 'The Prospector' between East Perth and Kalgoorlie, the AvonLink between Midland (Helena Street) and Northam, and the Merredin-Link between Perth and Merredin.

Transwa also operate coaches to many destinations, including Albany, Augusta, Bunbury, Esperance, Kalbarri, Geraldton, Pemberton and others.

4WD vehicles are a good idea in the outback

Ferries

Ferries serve travel between Elizabeth Quay and Mends Street Jetty on the south bank of the Swan; and sail from Barrack Street Jetty (next to Elizabeth Quay) to Fremantle (Victoria Quay) and Rottnest Island. Ferries also travel to Rottnest from Hillarys Yacht Club and North Fremantle (Rous Head). There are three ferry operators: Rottnest Express (tel: 1300 467 688; www.rottnestex press.com.au; departs from Fremantle and Perth City); Rottnest Fast Ferries (tel: 08-9246 1039; www.rottnestfast-ferries.com.au; departs from Hillary's Ferry Terminal); and SeaLink Rottnest Island (tel: 08-9325 9352; www.seal inkrottnest.com.au).

Taxis

All taxis in WA have metres operated by distance and time, which is connected to a rooftop light that illuminates when the cab is vacant. Cabs can be booked either by phone or online. Hailing of taxis on the street is permitted in WA. There are also taxi ranks at airports, many railway stations, popular nightspots and shopping centres. 'Silver Service' taxis will charge more. Taxis normally carry only four passengers, but maxi-cabs, which take six to 10 passengers, are available on request. Smoking is banned in all cabs, and the passenger may be fined if not wearing a seatbelt. To book a cab (just about anywhere in Australia) tel: 131 008.

Car hire

International car-hire companies offer good discounts on pre-booked hires, with the option to return the vehicle to another major centre at no extra charge. The minimum age for hiring a car is 18, but drivers under 25 pay a surcharge. A national driving licence is acceptable if it is written in English; otherwise you should obtain an international driver's licence. If your picture ID is not on the licence, you may have to produce your passport. Insurance on conventional rental cars is invalid on unsealed (dirt) roads, but most hire companies insure 4WD vehicles for any road that is shown on a map. Cover for single-vehicle accidents is subject to a high excess payment. Major international car-rental firms include:

Avis (tel: 13 63 33; www.avis.com.au)
Budget (tel: 1300 362 848; www.budget.com.au)
Europcar (tel: 1300 131 390; www.europcar.com.au)
Hertz (tel: 13 30 39; www.hertz.com.au)
Thrifty (tel: 1300 367 227; www.thrifty.com.au)

Driving

Traffic drives on the left in Australia, so you usually give way to the right and road signs usually match international rules. There is a 0.05 percent blood alcohol limit for drivers, which is widely enforced by the practice of random breath tests. Police also conduct random drug tests – both involve stopping entire lanes of traffic, or even whole roads.

Australian resident visa and immigration stamping tool

Off-road driving

When driving on sand it is always advisable to carry a 'snatch strap' in the event of getting bogged in loose sand. Check with your 4WD hire company that you have one in your vehicle. Also consult them for the correct tyre pressure for your vehicle.

V

Visas and passports

Your passport must be valid for at least six months from your date of arrival into Australia. All non-Australian citizens need a valid visa to enter Australia, with the exception of New Zealand citizens travelling on New Zealand passports, who are issued with a visa on arrival in Australia. Visas are available from Australian visa offices such as Australian embassies, high commissions and consulates, and from travel agents and airlines in some countries.

The **Electronic Transfer Authority** (ETA) enables visitors to obtain a visa on the spot from their travel agent or airline office. The system is in place in over 30 countries, including the UK and the US. ETA visas are generally valid over a 12-month period; single stays must not exceed three months, but return visits within the 12-month period are allowed. ETAs are issued free, or you can purchase one online for A\$20 from www.eta.immi.gov.au.

Most EU citizens are eligible for an **eVisitor** visa, which is free and can be obtained online. **Tourist visas** are available for continuous stays longer than three months, but must be obtained from an Australian visa office, such as an embassy or consulate. A A\$20 fee applies. Those travelling on any kind of tourist visa are not permitted to work while in Australia.

Working Holiday Visas are obtainable for citizens of some countries (including the United Kingdom, Canada, France, Germany, the Netherlands and Ireland) who are between the ages of 18 and 31.

The concept behind the visa is to encourage cultural exchange and closer ties between Australia and eligible countries. People must be outside Australia when they apply for their first Working Holiday visa and when the visa is decided. The initial period of the visa is 12 months, but in certain circumstance (such as if the visa holder spends a period working in a rural area where there is a labour shortage) it can be extended for a further year. For more information, visit the website: www.immi.gov.au/Visas/Pages/417.aspx

W

Weights and measures

Australia uses the metric system. Women's clothes are labelled in the UK way – sizes 8, 10, 12, etc, or simply as small, medium, large, etc. Shoes may be in UK or European sizes. In pubs some old-fashioned beer measures cling on: a pony is a very small glass; schooner is a bit bigger; midi is biggest, about half a pint. 'Small' and 'large' glasses (roughly half-pint and pint) are used in some establishments.

BOOKS AND FILM

Few places on the planet are as scantily populated or have a landscape as diverse and dramatic as Western Australia, and the state's oceans and outback have inspired writers and provided endless epic backdrops for many cinematic scenes. This is a place where the horizon is broad, the sky massive and the stars burn bright. Its immensity encourages the imagination to run wild. Narratives have permeated this land for millennia, growing in fantastic detail as they descended from the Dreamtime through generations of storytellers, relating tales around campfires. Today you can still hear those tales, told by people who have been custodians of this continent for more than 40,000 years. And you can also dig into a rich seam of modern stories, works of art by people such as Tim Winton, which convey a sense of what life is really like in this unique corner of the world.

Books

Not many authors have captured a sense of place quite as completely as the multi award-winning writer Tim Winton has managed to do with his sunburnt, ocean-soaked oeuvre of books set, primarily, in his homeland of Western Australia. Winton was born in Perth, but spent many of his formative years in Albany, after the family moved to the South Pacific–facing town when he was 12.

Winton is a keen surfer and environmentalist, and ocean waves wash through his work, which submerges the reader into the sea and landscape of Western Australia and burns with a relentless shimmering heat that anyone who has spent time here will recognise. Every one of his 12 novels published to date are well worth seeking out, but as a literary backdrop to your time in WA, his 2001 novel *Dirt Music* is an excellent starter. Also dive into his debut work *An Open Swimmer* (1982) as well as *Cloudstreet* (1991) and *Breath* (2008). *The Shark Net* by Robert Drewe is a beautifully written autobiographical account of a childhood spent in Perth's suburbs during the 1950s, when the sunny city was cast into shade by a series of murders. Drewe has also authored numerous excellent stories and novels exploring Western Australian society and the formative role the landscape plays in shaping it, including *The Savage Crows*, *A Cry in the Jungle Bar*, *The Bodysurfers*, *Fortune*, *The Bay of Contented Men*, *Our Sunshine*, *The Drowner*, *Grace* and *The Rip*.

Other notable works by Western Australian writers include the award-winning 1937 novel *The Young Desire It* by Perth author Seaforth Mackenzie, who also wrote *Dead Men Rising* about the bloody Cowra breakout (when Japa-

John Jarratt in Wolf Creek 2

nese prisoners of war staged a dramatic escape from a World War II POW camp), an incident that Mackenzie experienced first-hand.

Western Australia has also produced the novelists Kim Scott – *Lost* (2006), *That Deadman Dance* (2010) and *Taboo* (2017) and Amanda Curtin – *The Sinkings* (2008) and *Elemental* (2013) – and the poet Tracy Ryan.

Film

Robert Drewe's book *Our Sunshine* was made into a 2003 film, retitled *Ned Kelly*, directed by Gregor Jordan and starring Western Australia's best-known actor Heath Ledger (*A Knight's Tale*, *Monster's Ball*, *Brokeback Mountain*, *The Dark Knight*) alongside compatriots Orlando Bloom, Naomi Watts and Geoffrey Rush.

The award-winning and internationally acclaimed film *Rabbit-Proof Fence* (2002) – directed by Phillip Noyce and starring Everlyn Sampi, Kenneth Branagh and David Gulpilil – is based on the book *Follow the Rabbit-Proof Fence* by Doris Pilkington Garimara. It traces the true story of the author's mother Molly who, with two other mixed-race girls (Daisy and Grace), ran away from the Moore River Native Settlement just north of Perth, to return to their Aboriginal families, after being forcibly placed there in 1931.

Also based on a true story and several books, (primarily one of the same name, written by Louis de Bernieres) the 2011 film *Red Dog* tells the tale of a charismatic kelpie/cattle dog cross famous for his travels through Western Australia's Pilbara region. A prequel, *Red Dog: True Blue* was released in 2016. A statue dedicated to the real Red Dog's memory can be found in Dampier (see page 101).

The disturbing Australian horror film *Wolf Creek* (2005), written and directed by Greg McLean and starring John Jarratt as a murderous psychopath who captures and tortures a trio of backpackers, begins in Broome and contains scenes set in Halls Creek and Wolfe Creek National Park, both in Western Australia (although the film was shot in South Australia). The original garnered both negative criticism and acclaim for its relentless intensity, grit and gore, but a rather unimaginative and disappointing sequel, *Wolf Creek 2*, came out in 2013.

In 2017, Tim Winton's novel Breath was made into a film starring Perth-born actor Rachael Blake (Lantana) and fellow Australians Simon Baker, Elizabeth Debicki and Richard Roxburgh.

ABOUT THIS BOOK

This *Explore Guide* has been produced by the editors of Insight Guides, whose books have set the standard for visual travel guides since 1970. With top-quality photography and authoritative recommendations, these guidebooks bring you the very best routes and itineraries in the world's most exciting destinations.

BEST ROUTES

The routes in the book provide something to suit all budgets, tastes and trip lengths. As well as covering the destination's many classic attractions, the itineraries track lesser-known sights, and there are also excursions for those who want to extend their visit outside the city. The routes embrace a range of interests, so whether you are an art fan, a gourmet, a history buff or have kids to entertain, you will find an option to suit.

We recommend reading the whole of a route before setting out. This should help you to familiarise yourself with it and enable you to plan where to stop for refreshments – options are shown in the 'food and drink' box at the end of each tour.

For our pick of the tours by theme, consult Recommended routes for… (see pages 6–7).

INTRODUCTION

The routes are set in context by this introductory section, giving an overview of the destination to set the scene, plus background information on food and drink, shopping and more, while a succinct history timeline highlights the key events over the centuries.

DIRECTORY

Also supporting the routes is a Directory chapter, with a clearly organised A–Z of practical information, our pick of where to stay while you are there and select restaurant listings; these eateries complement the more low-key cafés and restaurants that feature within the routes and are intended to offer a wider choice for evening dining. Also included here are some nightlife listings and our recommendations for books and films about the destination.

ABOUT THE AUTHORS

This book was written by Patrick Kinsella, a freelance journalist and editor origionally from the busy built-up streets of southeast England – which explains why he enjoys exploring the vast and isolated region of Western Australia. A dual citizen of the United Kingdom and Australia, Patrick has also worked on *Insight Guides Explore Sydney, Fiji, Melbourne, Queensland and New Zealand.*

CONTACT THE EDITORS

We hope you find this Explore Guide useful, interesting and a pleasure to read. If you have any questions or feedback on the text, pictures or maps, please do let us know. If you have noticed any errors or outdated facts, or have suggestions for places to include on the routes, we would be delighted to hear from you. Please drop us an email at hello@insightguides.com. Thanks!

CREDITS

Explore Perth & West Coast Australia
Editor: Sian Marsh
Author: Patrick Kinsella
Head of DTP and Pre-Press: Rebeka Davies
Managing Editor: Carine Tracanelli
Picture Manager: Tom Smyth
Picture Editor: Aude Vauconsant
Cartography: Carte
Photo credits: Alamy 4/5T, 18, 22, 44, 45, 46, 50B, 54B, 55L, 66, 69, 70, 74B, 77, 98/99, 108/109T, 110, 111, 112/113, 114, 115, 116/117, 124/125, 126, 138, 139; AWL Images 1; Cameron Perry/ The Boatshed 37; Danica Zuks/Balthazar 118/119; Fraser's 120/121; Getty Images 4ML, 10, 11, 12, 15, 19, 24, 25, 26, 27L, 26/27, 54T, 58B, 76, 82/83, 96T, 100/101, 108MC, 108MC, 108ML, 131L; iStock 4ML, 4MC, 4MR, 4MR, 4MC, 6TL, 6MC, 6ML, 6BC, 7T, 7MR, 7M, 7MR, 8ML, 8MC, 8ML, 8MC, 8MR, 8MR, 8/9T, 13L, 12/13, 14, 20, 20/21, 23, 28ML, 28MC, 28MR, 28ML, 28MC, 28MR, 28/29T, 30/31, 32/33, 34, 35, 36, 38, 39MC, 39T, 38/39T, 40, 41L, 40/41, 42, 43, 46/47, 48/49, 52, 54/55, 56, 57, 60T, 60B, 61, 64T, 65, 72, 73, 75L, 79, 80, 81, 84, 85L, 84/85, 86/87, 89L, 90/91, 92/93, 94, 95, 96B, 97, 98, 102, 103, 104, 105, 106/107, 108ML, 108MR, 122, 123, 127, 128, 129, 130, 130/131, 132/133, 135L, 134/135, 136, 137; Shutterstock 16/17, 21L, 53, 58/59T, 62/63, 64B, 67, 68, 71, 74T, 74/75, 78, 88, 88/89, 99L, 134; Subiaco Arts Centre 51B; Subiaco Museum 50/51T; The Hummus Club 47L, 108MR
Cover credits: Shutterstock (main&bottom)

Every effort has been made to provide accurate information in this publication, but changes are inevitable. The publisher cannot be responsible for any resulting loss, inconvenience or injury.

DISTRIBUTION

UK, Ireland and Europe
Apa Publications (UK) Ltd
sales@insightguides.com
United States and Canada
Ingram Publisher Services
ips@ingramcontent.com
Australia and New Zealand
Woodslane
info@woodslane.com.au
Southeast Asia
Apa Publications (Singapore) Pte
singaporeoffice@insightguides.com
Worldwide
Apa Publications (UK) Ltd
sales@insightguides.com

SPECIAL SALES, CONTENT LICENSING AND COPUBLISHING

Insight Guides can be purchased in bulk quantities at discounted prices. We can create special editions, personalised jackets and corporate imprints tailored to your needs.
sales@insightguides.com
www.insightguides.biz

Printed by CTPS – China
All Rights Reserved
© 2019 Apa Digital (CH) AG and
Apa Publications (UK) Ltd
First Edition 2019

INDEX

A

Aberdeen Street Heritage Precinct 47
Aboriginal Art Gallery 33
Aboriginal Interpretation Centre 81
Albany 86
Ancient Empire Walk 86
Aquarium of Western Australia 66
Armadale 80
Art Gallery of Western Australia 44
Augusta 85
Avon Valley 91

B

Balingup 87
Barracks Gateway 33
Barrack Square 30
Barrack Street Jetty 30
Batavia 95
Battye Library of Western Australian History 45
Beagle Bay 104
Belmont Park Racecourse 55
Bibbulmun Track 81
Blue Room Theatre 46
Boorabbin National Park 91
Botanic Gardens 32
Bottle Bay 96
Brass Monkey 46
Breakers 89
Bridgetown 87
Brighton Beach 65
Broadwalk 32
Broome 103
Buccaneer Archipelago 106
Bunbury 82
Bungle Bungle Range 107
Burswood Park 55
Busselton 83

C

Cable Beach 104
Cape Leeuwin Lighthouse 85
Cape Le Grand National Park 90
Cape Leveque 104
Cape Naturaliste 84
Cape Range National Park 101
Cape-to-Cape Walk 84
Carnarvon 98
Caversham Wildlife Park 75
Cenotaph 32
Central Greenough Historical Settlement 93
Cinema Paradiso 46
City Beach 64
Claisebrook Cove 52
Coral Bay 99
Corner Gallery 49
Cottesloe 63
Cottesloe Reef Fish Habitat Protection Area 63
Council House 39
Crown Perth 55
Cultural Centre 44

D

Dampier 101
Decoy 37
Denham 96
Denmark 86
Derby 106
Diamond Tree 86
Dirk Hartog Island 97
Discovery and Visitor Centre 96
DNA Tower 32
Dunsborough 84
Dwellingup 87

E

Eagles Heritage Wildlife Centre 85
East Perth Public Art Walk 53
Eco Abrolhos Tours 95
Edgecombe Brothers 76
Edith Cowan Clocktower 33
Elizabeth Quay 31
Elizabeth Quay Bridge 31
Esperance 90
Exmouth 99
Navy Pier 99

F

Ferguson Valley 87
First Contact sculpture 31
Fitzgerald River National Park 89
Floreat Beach 65
food and drink 16
Forest Heritage Centre 87
Forrest Chase 42
Francois Peron National Park 96
Fred Jacoby Forest Park 81
Fremantle
Fremantle Doctor 66

G

Geikie Gorge 106
Geraldton 93
Gloucester National Park 86
Gloucester Park 54
Gomboc Gallery Sculpture Park 77
Government House 39
Great Ocean Drive 90
Guildford 72
Gunyulgup Galleries 84

H

Halls Creek 107
Hamelin Pool 97
Hangover Bay 93
Hannans North Tourist Mine 91
Hay Street Mall 42
Hearson's Cove 101
Heath Ledger Theatre 46
Heirisson Island 35
Henley Park Winery 76
Hillary's Boat Harbour 66
Hippo's Yawn 89
His Majesty's Theatre 42

History Village **81**
HMAS Perth **86**
Hopetoun **89**
Hotham Valley Tourist
    Railway **87**
Houghton Wines **77**
Houtman Abrolhos Islands **95**
Humps **89**
Hyden **88**

I

Illa Kurri Sacred Dreaming
    Path **53**
Ironbark Brewery **74**

J

Jewel Cave **85**
John Forrest National Park **77**
John Miller Design **84**

K

Kalamunda **81**
Kalbarri **96**
Kalbarri National Park **96**
Kalgoorlie **90**
Kangaroo Point **93**
Karijini **102**
Karratha **101**
King Sound **106**
Kings Park **31**
King Street Precinct **42**

L

Lake Cave **85**
Lake MacLeod **99**
Lake Monger **49**
Lake Thetis **93**
Lamont Winery **76**
Lancaster Wines **74**
Lancelin **92**
Landing, the **33**
Leighton Beach **63**
Lesueur National Park **93**
Little Beach **87**
Lombadina **104**
Lotterywest Federation

Walkway **32**
Lucky Bay **90**
Lycopod Island **32**

M

Maalinup Aboriginal Gallery
    76
Malcolm Douglas Crocodile
    Park and Animal Refuge
    104
Mammoth Cave **85**
Mandurah **78**
Mandurah Crab Festival **80**
Mann Winery **76**
Margaret River **84**
Margaret River Chocolate
    Company **74**
Margaret River Visitor
    Centre **85**
Market Square **49**
Marmion Beach **66**
Marmion Marine Park **65**
Matagarup Bridge **54**
Mends Street Jetty **36**
Metro City **46**
Middle Lagoon **104**
Monkey Mia **97**
Mosman Beach **63**
Motor Museum **88**
Mueller Park **49**

N

Nambung National Park **93**
Nanarup Beach **86**
Naturaliste Charters **85**
New Norcia **102**
New Subiaco **49**
Ningaloo Marine
    Interactions **99**
Northbridge **46**
North Cottesloe Beach **64**

O

Old Court House **39**
Old Gaol **45**
Old Perth Fire Station **42**

Old Perth Observatory **33**
Old Railway Station
    Museum **91**
One Arm Point **105**
Onslow **101**

P

Parliament of Western
    Australia **33**
Pemberton **85**
Perth Concert Hall **40**
Perth Institute of
    Contemporary Art **46**
Perth Mint **40**
Perth's Moonlight Cinema
    32
Perth Stadium **54**
Perth Stadium Station **55**
Perth Zoo **37**
Piazza Nanni **47**
Pilbara **101**
Pinnacles Desert **93**
Pinnaroo Point **67**
Pioneer Cemetery **53**
Pioneer Women's Memorial
    32
Plateia Helias **47**
Point Fraser **35**
Port Beach **62**
Port Hedland **101**
Purnululu National Park
    107

Q

Queen's Gardens **54**

R

Regal Theatre **50**
Reptile and Wildlife Centre
    80
Rockingham **78**
Rokeby Road **50**
Rotary **90**
Rottnest **68**
Royal Perth Hospital **41**
Russell Square **46**

S

Salvation Army building **42**
Scarborough **65**
Scarborough to Trigg Heritage Walk **65**
Scotsdale Tourist Drive **86**
Sculpture by the Sea **64**
Serpentine Falls **80**
Serpentine National Park **80**
Shark Bay Marine Park **96**
Shell Beach **96**
Signature Ring **34**
Sorrento Beach **66**
South Beach **62**
South Cottesloe Beach **63**
Space and Technology Museum **98**
State Library **45**
State Tennis Centre **55**
State Theatre Centre **46**
State War Memorial **32**
St George's Cathedral **39**
Stirling Gardens **38**
St Mary's Cathedral **41**
Stokes Inlet National Park **90**
Subiaco Arts Centre **51**
Subiaco Museum **51**
Subiaco Oval **49**
Subiaco Square **48**
Supreme Court Gardens **38**
Supreme Court of Western Australia **39**
Swan Bells **30**
Swanbourne Beach **64**

T

Talijancich Winery **76**
Taste the South Winery Tours **84**
Theatre Gardens **50**
The Deanery **39**
The Duxton **40**
Titles Office **42**
Toodyay **91**
Torndirrup National Park **86**
Town Hall **42**
Trigg Beach **65**
Tunnel Creek National Park **106**
Twilight Cove **90**
Two People's Bay **87**

U

University of Western Australia **32**
Urban Orchard **44**

V

Valley of the Giants Treetop Walk **86**
Vasse Felix **85**
Victoria Gardens **53**
Vietnam Memorial **32**
Voyager Estate **85**

W

WACA **54**
Walpole **86**
Wardan Aboriginal Cultural Centre **84**
Warren National Park **86**
Waterbank **54**
Water Garden Pavilion **32**
Watermans Beach **66**
Wave Rock **88**
Wesley Quarter **42**
Western Australian Museum **45**
Western Australia Rowing Club **35**
Wetlands **90**
Whitfords Beach **67**
Whitfords Nodes **67**
Windjana Gorge National Park **106**
Wolfe Creek **107**
Wollemi Pine **32**
Wula Gura Eco Cultural Adventures **97**
Wyndham **107**

Y

Yagan Memorial Park **76**
Yagan Square **42**
Yagan statue **35**
Yalgorup National Park **80**
Yallingup **84**
Yallingup Galleries **84**
Yallingup Ngilgi Cave **85**
Yamaji Drive Trail **95**
Yardie Creek Gorge **101**
York **88**

MAP LEGEND

●	Start of tour
→	Tour & route direction
❶	Recommended sight
❷	Recommended restaurant/café
★	Place of interest
❶	Tourist information
---	Ferry route
✈	Airport
🚌	Main bus station
✉	Main post office
✚	Hospital
Ⓜ	Museum
📖	Library
✝	Church
⚲	Lighthouse
☀	Viewpoint
↶	Beach
	Important building
	Transport hub
	Park
	Pedestrian area
	Urban area